KEEP AT IT

Rev. Walter A. Jackson III

ISBN: 1542534062
ISBN 13: 9781542534062

FOREWORD 1

It is my pleasure to have had the opportunity to read and respond to the book *Keep At It*, by Rev. Walter A. Jackson III. This writing covers a wide range of endeavors. It is my thinking that this autobiography is inspirational. He has dealt with the matter of growing up in a very interesting environment. While there is a multiplicity of incidents covered in the writing, the emphasis remains on integration rather than separation, in terms of outcomes.

This is not a how-to book. It shows, however, how everyone profits when each person involved is truly committed to a worthwhile process. To my way of thinking, this concept very closely follows the dictum, "A rising tide lifts all boats."

The readers, throughout the book, are constantly faced with the reality of examining their own humanity and outlook. Throughout the book, the readers encounter opportunities to make choices. The constant message seems to be that sometimes the most direct way may not be the best way for one to go. There are times that one may want to slow down or travel in a different direction.

At this juncture in our national existence, as we are undergoing internal queries and realignments as to the proper way to go, this book provides an opportunity to reflect on the many alternatives. The central core of *Keep At It* is that most problems that initially look unsolvable will yield to sustained, concerted attack if there is an honest desire to come up with a solution that is palatable as well as humanely centered.

Thanks for the opportunity to share. This is a fine work. God bless and keep you and yours.

Dr. Donald F. Taylor Sr.

Pastor Emeritus, Greater Mount Zion Baptist Church, Chesapeake, Virginia

Assistant Pastor, Wainwright Baptist Church, Charles Town, West Virginia

FOREWORD 2

Let me introduce you to the man behind the book that you are opening.

Rev. Walter A. Jackson III burst into my life like a comet in February 1996 at a huge (forty thousand attendees) pastors' gathering at the Georgia Dome in Atlanta.

Having arrived alone from my home far away and having no idea what to expect, I realized that I had neglected to reserve a place to stay or even a rental car. Dependent on public transportation, I rode the rails from that gigantic, impersonal airport to the big hotels near the venue, hoping to rent out a part of a room occupied by pastors.

Once I was settled in, I made my way to the stadium. Promise Keepers was hosting the event, and as a Scandinavian American Lutheran, I was pretty far off the "reservation" and exploring some unknown territory in an exuberant, evangelical environment. Granted, I've always had some incurable Pentecostal tendencies, so perhaps the Holy Spirit was drawing me there.

Pastors tend to sing loudly with big baritone voices, and you can imagine that tens of thousands of them singing "Mighty Fortress" can stir the blood. A lot. During the first session, they announced tryouts for a gospel choir that would back up the main singers. I had no business attending any such audition, but hey, they offered free T-shirts and dinner to those who did, so I showed up. We had to sing a cappella for some Nashville record exec, one at a time, and the only gospel song I knew was "Go down, Moses." Gave it a shot. By the grace of God, they let me in, and we started singing backup to the main worship leaders on the stage, in front of a sea of pastors.

The speakers started addressing the prickly issue of race relations. Never having had any meaningful connection with persons of color, I assumed I had no racist inclinations. I started to get bored and went out into the big concrete stadium hallway (where all the concessions are) and sat down next to a pillar.

It was then that the Lord spoke to me. "How do you feel about African Americans?"

"No problem Lord. Everyone's the same to me."

"Really?"

"Yes. I'm not a racist. Never use the *N* word."

"Look inside your heart." (This is where it gets strange, and a "vision" started.)

"No one can 'see' inside his heart, Lord."

"Look, I told you!"

"OK, then." So I looked and saw a cold, heavy rock filling my heart.

"Reach down into your heart, grab the stone, pull it out, and throw it as hard as you can."

So I did. I threw it as far as I could. Then I burst into tears.

The Lord—the Holy Spirit "speaking" to my spirit—said, "This cold rock is how you view black brothers and sisters. You have no love for them. You don't hate them and do not speak ill of them, but you are cold as a rock to them. From now on, you will be different."

I found my way back into the crowded arena. I don't remember anything between that transformative moment and our singing debut as a gospel choir, backing up Steve Green. We were standing on risers behind Steve, who was belting out "Let the Walls Fall Down," which became the anthem of the gathering.

What happened next wasn't much different from what happened at that first Pentecost. The place disintegrated. Forty thousand Christian leaders, lit up by the Holy Spirit, found themselves in "dog piles" of prayer with strangers. Weeping, praying spontaneously, speaking in tongues, prophesying—and all this with strangers who happened to be seated around them. Restoring order was more or less impossible.

I found myself, literally, in a pile of weeping men from the choir. Racial hatred and separation was being broken as we all sought out people who looked different than we did.

I ended up praying with Walter Jackson, and the rest is history. For the past twenty years, we have been in continuous contact, despite the fact that we serve small churches on opposite coasts of the country. We have prayed each other through tough times and celebrated the occasional victory together.

One of the highlights was having Walter lead the 450,000 listeners of my afternoon drive-time radio show in singing "Lift Every Voice and Sing," the black national anthem, and explaining the history of the song to my audience in Los Angeles, the Bay Area, and Sacramento.

The recent advent of podcasting has been a great blessing to many around the world. I would make a guess that Walter's sermons are more popular among my congregants here at Robinwood Church than mine are. It's hard to know for sure, with over three hundred thousand small churches in America, but I would be very surprised if Walter were not the most gifted communicator of the gospel in any "non mega" church from coast to coast. As with Van Gogh, who became famous only after his lifetime, whoever curates Walter Jackson's sermons in the future will possess an American cultural treasure to share with yet-unborn generations.

His preaching and singing has authentic and profound roots in the African American experience, but they are, for some reason, especially accessible to those unfamiliar with black Christianity. His work is universal in appeal.

Enjoy reading and savoring the story of a quintessentially American life.

David Housholder
Senior Pastor, Robinwood Church, Huntington Beach, California,
Author of *Light Your Church on Fire without Burning It Down,*
The Blackberry Bush, Seven Secrets to a Meaningful Life,
and *Own Your Life*

PREFACE

Having always loved stories, I was delighted to hear in the adult conversations that children were not supposed to be privy to the stories of "the good ole days," "the hard-time days," and the stories of the horrors and hardships of the Great Depression and the pre integration Deep South as well as the subtleties of northern segregation that were not quite as obvious. As a child, I positioned myself to hear some of these stories even though children were forbidden to be in "grown folk's conversation." As a quiet, introverted loner, I learned to be still, to listen, and to see things that many other children had no clue were going on. My family considered me an unusual child because I was always so serious. My aunt Cynthia (Aunt Cinnie) used to say I was the oldest little child she had ever known. However, that characteristic allowed me to learn a lot about life and to observe situations and know what the outcomes would be.

As an adult, I continued to observe people. When I was a bus operator in Washington, DC, I would watch people's interactions on the bus, at intersections, and at stoplights. I learned a great deal about the nature of people and their nonverbal communication and body language. I did this in my family and ministry, as well. I am writing this book with the hope that it will help others in some way to maintain in faith in themselves, their dreams, their goals, and most of all, in Christ.

I would like to thank my friend and former coworker, Steven, who gladly volunteered to do the first edit of each chapter, giving honest criticism and thoughts. I pray that he "keeps at it" as he works through setbacks and obstacles in life, as all of us have. Thank you.

Thank you to my family; my birth daughter, Melanie Renee, and my son, Daniel whom I adopted while he was in foster care in my home. They have both been through a great deal and have landed and will land on their feet. Daddy loves you both and always will.

Thank you to my sister Cynthia. We have become best friends and spiritually connected. Thank you to my cousins, those I mention in this book and those I do not, for your support as a family. (Jay and Carol Graham, you were not yet born when most of this story unfolded, but I thank you for being a part of our loving family.)

Thank you to my uncle Glenn Graham, who filled in some missing pieces that helped me connect some of the dots from Youngstown.

Most of all, I thank my dad, Walter A. Jackson Jr. You are the rock that has kept me going so many times when I wanted to give up.

Thank you to my pastor friends/encouragers. Dr. Donald F. Taylor, my assistant pastor (with whom I joke, "When I grow up, I want to be just like you!") suggested the title from the story about my grandmother, who told me, "Keep at it."

Thank you to Rev. James D. Holland of the Lovely Valley Baptist Church, who showed me what courage is when he lost his wife and stood strong to deliver her eulogy. You have been a great friend and pastoral example to me during my thirty-six years as a pastor in the Brackett-Morrell Association.

Thank you to Dr. James Harrison, executive minister of the American Baptist Churches of the South. You have inspired me with your wisdom so many times over the last few years. For that, I am eternally grateful! You know just what to say at the right place and at the right time to inspire people.

Thank you to Dr. Earl Beeks and Dr. Esther Beeks for your friendship over the years. You two, along with Rev. Dr. Betty Lancaster Short and the late Bishop Stephen Short, are my oldest friends.

To my friend Bishop Scottie Jackson: in a short time, you have become a true friend and encourager in the things of the Lord. The scripture verses you send daily are a gentle reminder to keep my focus on the things of the Lord. Each verse that you have texted to me has been just what I needed that day. Only the Holy Ghost can do that.

Thank you to Mike and Connie Adams and Russell and Debra Low for befriending me when I moved to West Virginia. You know the part you played in getting me through some difficult times. I believe your friendship helped to pull me through some very dark days.

Thank you, Elvin (Bob) Shanholtz. When I read your poetry on that poetry website and wrote to you and you came to hear me preach, I was honored to help you through the loss of your wife to cancer. You helped me through a very difficult time in my life as well by encouraging me to hang in there ("keep at it") when I felt like throwing in the towel. Through you, your family members have also become my friends. I hope that you will publish your poetry; the world needs to see and hear it! (Hint! Hint! Hint!)

Thank you, David Housholder, my friend and prayer partner. If I had not gone to that Pastors' Promise Keepers Meeting in Atlanta, we never would have met. We would not have been prayer partners, and there is so much encouragement we would not have given to each other. It all started with being chosen to sing "Let the Walls Come Down" in the choir. Thank you, my brother from another mother. You were also the doorway to the global exposure of my sermons and to the publishing of this book.

Thank you, Regina T. Jackson, for our laughs and for our conversations on forgiveness, growth in Christ, healing, and the love of children and grandchildren.

The beauty of all this is that "When We All Get to Heaven", we will all meet, share forever, rejoice forever, sing forever, praise forever, and just keep at it!

1

THE EXTENDED FAMILY BLESSING

N o experience has a bigger impact on one's life than having a nurturing, loving, caring, and affirming extended family. Your core values and beliefs have their roots within that family structure. Every joy, every sorrow, every moment of discipline, every moment of praise, worship, play, and even crisis write deeply into your soul and spirit the codes that programmed you to be you.

At 5:25 p.m. on June 21, the longest day of 1950, I was welcomed into the Jackson/Graham family as the second grandchild on both sides of the family. Daddy made a phone call from the pay phone at Freedmen's Hospital near Howard University in Washington, DC, to Granddaddy and Grandma Jackson across town and to Grandma Graham in Youngstown, Ohio. From there, the word spread to the rest of the family that I would soon become endeared to and that, in my mind, was the best family in the whole world! Nana, my father's paternal grandmother; Aunt Belle, her sister and my great-great aunt; two grandfathers; two grandmothers; and other great aunts and great uncles on both sides of the family were the elders. Now, I think of them as the elders of the tribes who sat at the village gates in Israel or the revered ones of the tribes in Africa. I would hang on to their every word and soak up the experiences they shared. To me they were royalty. They were *my* royalty.

From family photographs, I learned how they had passed me around as an infant and dressed up and sat together for portraits with me as an infant. The message that sent to me was that they valued my life. They saw me as special and as an important part of the family. They didn't just see me as important to them. They saw my sister and all of my cousins as important to the family. That message was made clear to each of us from the moment of our birth. Each of us was held, cuddled, talked to, kissed, hugged, and tossed in the air and caught, which brought our laughter, as we learned to trust them. We were disciplined, when it was needed. We were sometimes deprived of things we enjoyed to teach us that there is a consequence when you do something wrong. We were made to feel "safe and secure from all alarms" to borrow a phrase from the hymn "Leaning on the Everlasting Arms."

The affirmation of my personhood was best felt at family gatherings. It was not just the Thanksgiving, Christmas, and Resurrection Sunday get-togethers that were special—I will talk about those in detail—but the general gatherings at the central location of Granddaddy and Grandma Jackson's house after church on Sunday or at our house or at Auntie and Uncle Sidney's just because we wanted to get together.

Sometimes just because we were (and are) family, we would go to Granddaddy and Grandma's house after church. We might have intended just to stop by to pick up homemade rolls for dinner at home, but we would stay to eat dinner there along with aunts, uncles, and cousins. We always had clothes there to put on after church. Nana, my great-grandmother (Granddaddy Jackson's mother), would have been dropped off from Metropolitan Baptist Church or would have walked from her house around the corner. Sometimes we would have picked up Aunt Belle, Nana's sister and my great-great aunt. They would make such a fuss over my sister, my cousins, and me, often digging into their change purses to give us nickels, dimes, and sometimes quarters. I fondly remember the wet kisses they gave that we always wiped off our cheeks once we were out of their sight and how they would come to our defense if they thought we were about to get spanked by our parents in their presence. Aunt Belle had a way of screaming that would send a shiver up your spine. Nana would jump and shout, "Aw, Lord!" It worked sometimes, getting us off with a stern warning from our parents or a "delay of judgment" until we got home.

Nana and Aunt Belle were the senior matriarchs (more like queen mothers). Though Aunt Belle had no children or grandchildren, she shared her sister's children, grandchildren, and great-grandchildren as though they were her own. I learned years later that Aunt Belle would ask my parents and my aunt and uncle what my cousins and my sister and I had asked Santa Claus for, and she would assist in making sure that Santa delivered. She would make trips downtown on the streetcar to Kann's, Lansburgh's, Woodward and Lothrop, and Hecht's department stores to make the purchases because she "wanted those children happy on Christmas Day." Nana would always have cards containing dollar bills or a silver dollar coin for each of us.

Those after-church gatherings were precious and priceless. We children would play on the back porch or in the basement until dinner was heated up. You didn't cook it on Sunday. It had been cooked on Saturday, so that all that had to be done on Sunday was to heat it up. Granddaddy would be listening to whatever ball game was on the radio, or he would be watching a game on the Philco television in the living room as he sat in his favorite chair. No one but Granddaddy sat in that chair. No one but Grandma sat in her spot on the sofa next to his chair, either.

When dinner was ready, the adults had their seats at the dining room table, the youngest child sat in the high chair that all of us children had used at some point. The rest of us children sat at a card table set up nearby, where we could be monitored. This is where we were taught to eat what was on our plates, that we got nothing to drink until we'd eaten our food, and that if we didn't finish our food, we would get no dessert. The table was always referred to as "the kids' table." The big aspiration was to grow up and sit at "the grown folks' table"—the table of the elders. At least, that is the way I thought of it. Even though I could not get into their conversations because they were "grown folks," they seemed to have so much fun. I had fun watching them and listening to them and learning from them. These were the people who looked out for me. These were the people who kept me safe. These people, I knew, *loved me.*

I learned several things from those days. The elderly are to be respected and revered. There is an order in family leadership that everyone respects. Every family member has value and has a responsibility to nurture and train the youth.

I shall always cherish those Sunday afternoons, when the days seemed to last so much longer and were full of enjoyment. When dinner was over, my grandmother, my mother, and Auntie would clear the table, wash the dishes, put food away, and fix bags of food for each of us to take home along with the rolls we that we *really* had just come over for. Then the dining room table became the game table for the adults, and the kids' table became the game table for us. Sometimes the adults would play pinochle, Parcheesi, or Monopoly. The children would play dominoes, chinese checkers, checkers, Candy Land, or old maid. Or we would fold up the table and play pick-up sticks, marbles, or jacks on the floor. These were all games that Grandma taught us how to play by getting down on the floor with us.

Raised in the Family Village

Granddaddy and Grandma Jackson were the patriarch and matriarch on the Jackson side. Any disputes stopped when Granddaddy spoke. I never heard my grandmother call him by his first name. She always called him "Jackson." To the children she would say, "Did you hear Granddaddy?"

Growing up in the Jackson family meant that any adult member of the family had the right to correct you. You had better respect him, too! I guess that today's children would think that we were abused. We were not. We were not abused by being held to standards then or now. To my knowledge, none of us was ever hit with a stick, a coat hanger, an ironing cord, or any other horrific thing you hear of today—and you sometimes heard of then. No one punched us, broke limbs, blackened eyes, or any of those things that today would be a social-service nightmare. I thank God for that.

There was a code of ethics for our family. It was never written down, but it was taught, and we all knew it.

The Jackson Children's Code of Ethics and Standards of Behavior (as I remember it) is as follows:

- All adults are to be respected (and that includes no rolling your eyes or sucking your teeth).
- You address adults as Mr., Miss, Mrs., Sir/Ma'am, Aunt, Uncle, Grandma, or Granddaddy.
- You *never* (zero tolerance) talk back to an adult—not even under your breath.
- You stay out of grown folks' conversations unless they include you in them.
- If you have a problem with a teacher or another adult, you remain respectful and let your parents handle it.
- How they handle it is *not your business*!
- You tell the truth!
- You are sent to school to learn, not to be a behavior problem. If you misbehave at school, there will be a serious price to pay at home. (You have no behavior disorder that can't be fixed at home!)
- Family business and discussions are just that—*family business.*
- In this family, we go to church, and you will go and behave. (Case closed.)
- Chores and homework are done *before* you go out to play.
- A job worth doing is worth doing well.
- You must be indoors when the streetlights come on.

These were the standards in the Jackson family. I guess you could say these were our Thirteen Commandments. However, they were pretty much the same ones that many of the kids I grew up around had.

Corporal punishment was rare. We all knew the rules. It was a last resort, but if warranted, it would be used. However, we liked being in good standing with our parents and grandparents. I hated to disappoint my parents. That meant I had also disappointed myself.

Any adult in the family could correct us. Grandma Jackson used to watch my sister, my cousins, and me when we were small, before she had her first heart attack in 1955. She would walk around all day with a dish towel on her shoulder. It never fell off, and she could grab it and swat you with that dish towel so quickly that I swear that is how kung fu was invented. It wouldn't really hurt, but it got your attention if you were not listening. Then she would make you sit down somewhere until she told you that you could get up. Today, I guess that would be called "time out" or "redirect." We did not want Grandma to tell our parents that she had to correct us. And unless she had to do it more than once, she never told our parents on us. I guess that was her unwritten law.

It was not always about rules and what we could not do. Grandma and Granddaddy took us places. They made us laugh, too. Grandma would look for her glasses, and they would be on top of her head. The first time I saw Granddaddy put his teeth in, I was standing in the bathroom, watching him shave. I don't remember the conversation we were having. I just remember him washing his hands, opening the case with his teeth in it, and putting them in his mouth.

I must have had a shocked expression on my face. "Granddaddy! How do you do that?" I said.

He laughed and said, "You try."

When he left for work in his black suit—he drove a limousine for a funeral home before and after he retired from the Government Printing Office—he looked back at me and smiled. I must have spent the next two hours pulling at my gums.

I remember Grandma saying, "Aw, Jackson! Why did you tell that child that? You know he believes everything you tell him!" Then she turned to me. "Walter, go wash your hands and stop pulling at your mouth. You'll get germs!" Grandma was always worried about us kids getting "germs."

One time, Granddaddy and Grandma took my sister, my cousins, and me to the beach. It was the day I realized that beaches were open during the week. I believe it was an outing of the James E. Reese American Legion post, of which my grandfather and father were members. Granddaddy, a World War I veteran, was post commander. My father, now ninety, is probably the oldest member of that post.

That trip was the only time I ever saw my grandmother in anything that looked like a bathing suit. It was actually more like a dress. She did not get in the water, but she kept control of her grandchildren from the sandy shore. If I remember correctly, Grandma had brought a clothesline that she tied around the waists of Cynthia (my sister) and DeLyse (my cousin) to keep them from going too far out and drowning. There was not too much danger of that because they didn't want to stay in the water very long. Karen and Ora Marie, DeLyse's sisters, had not yet been born. Grandma made it clear that my cousin Vernon (who was eight years my senior) and I were not to go too far out.

Granddaddy played horseshoes with the men. Grandma took us on the kiddie rides.

Of course, when we got home, Grandma gave us all a bath. She didn't want us getting germs. Mind you, she had carried a bottle of rubbing alcohol to the beach to use before the picnic and in case of mosquitoes, which was another one of her concerns for her grandchildren.

Grandma Jackson, a.k.a. Dr. Hong Kong

Grandma was also the unofficial dentist as we started to lose our baby teeth. Somewhere along the way, we gave her the affectionate name of Dr. Hong Kong when she was getting ready to pull a loose tooth, or tend to a scraped knee or anything else that required a bandage. Of course, we would always laugh. If we were sick and could not go to school, we went to stay with Grandma, taking along whatever medicine Dr. Owens had prescribed. Dr. Hong Kong would administer it.

Pulling teeth was Grandma Jackson's (or should I say, Dr. Hong Kong's) area of specialization. It was a spectator sport for the rest of us children who had no loose teeth. This was usually a morning operation, and it started with the declaration that there was a "loose tooth among us." We cousins all would carry the kitchen step stool into the dining room, where there was the most light. One of us could easily have brought the stool in, but what fun would that have been? After all, we needed to be Dr. Hong Kong's assistants during this delicate procedure. The candidate for tooth removal would sit on the step stool. Grandma would look through her bifocals at the lose tooth and wiggle it with her finger to see if it was ready. We would hold our breath in suspense. Would this be a finger pull or a string pull operation? Only Dr. Hong Kong's expert hands and eyes could tell. We would move in close, sometimes looking over her shoulder. She was a short, thin lady, weighing only ninety pounds. She would tell us to give her room, and we would back up. Sometimes just the wiggling would do the trick. Sometime she would need to get some string to tie around the tooth to pull it.

Once the tooth was out, we would all pass it around and inspect it. We would need to see it from every angle and side. You don't get to see a sibling's or a cousin's tooth out of his or her head on a regular basis. Grandma would make the owner of that tooth gargle with salt-water after the procedure. We all would then inspect the hole where the tooth used to be. By this time, it would be almost lunchtime. Grandma had kept us entertained and occupied for several hours. She would then have us wash our hands so we wouldn't get germs.

Nana: Harriet (Hattie Burrell Jackson)

Nana never liked being called "grandma" and never used Harriet. She always went by Hattie. I did not know until after she died that she liked plays and that she had known Frederick Douglas who had sponsored her in a play. I discovered this one day when my dad saw on the news that when a school in Southeast DC was being renovated, workers found old theater tickets and playbills introducing a Hattie Burrell in a light fixture. I was living in West Virginia then, and I called the news station in DC. I told an editor that Hattie Burrell was my great-grandmother and that her two grandchildren were alive. I gave him my father's and aunt's phone numbers and addresses and sent a picture of her when she was in her twenties. As a result, Nana's only two grandchildren were on the evening news proudly talking about their grandmother who had known Frederick Douglass. I have had many great moments in my life, but that ranks as the proudest. I was able to give my father and my aunt a moment of fame. I have the interview on videotape. I plan to transfer it to a DVD. In death, my Nana got a moment in the spotlight.

My Great-Grandmother and Grandmother

It was also fun to watch Nana and Grandma Jackson on Tuesday nights as they watched wrestling on television. I really wasn't into the show. I was into watching my grandma Jackson and her mother-in-law (Nana) get into that show. Sometimes I would go into hysterics, laughing at them. Together, these two thin ladies did not weigh two hundred and ten pounds.

Nana would walk around the corner from her house on Tuesday evening after she had finished her dinner and evening chores to watch the show with Grandma. Grandma would have dessert ready. It would always be something good like peaches, homemade tapioca, ginger bread, pound cake, Breyers ice cream (when half a gallon of ice cream *was* half a gallon of ice cream) or a homemade pie.

They would watch the matches one after another. They had their favorite wrestlers and the ones they did not like. There were also referees they didn't like. They would sit there intently watching the TV screen, balling their fists, twisting their bodies, moving their thin arms, and grunting. "Mumma! Did you see that?" Grandma would yell.

"Rebecca! That referee makes me sick!" Nana would shout.

When their favorite wrestler, a black wrestler named Bobo Brazil, was in the ring with someone they didn't like, they would both jump up, run up to the twelve-inch, black-and-white television set with their fists balled up, and yell, "Get him, Bobo! Give him a coco butt to the head! That's it!"

At any moment, it seemed as if the television airwaves would reach out and consume the two of them. One time, Nana used me to demonstrate one of Bobo's moves. She grabbed me by my shoulders and pushed me onto the sofa. It shocked Grandma and me. I laughed until I cried. Grandma wasn't much better. I didn't know that little lady had that kind of strength. When she walked home that night, Grandma had me walk her to the corner while she watched from the porch. I waited as Nana walked to the end of the block and up the steps to her front porch, thinking that the way she and Grandma fought at the TV, no one would dare bother either of them.

I never thought of them as elderly and lacking vitality. That taught me that just because you have a few years on you does not mean you lack gusto. I hope I never lose my youthful luster and vitality for life, even if my body slows down. I want to stay as full of life as my two grandmothers and my great-grandmother were. I hope to have the dignity of my grandfather and the humor, courage, and strength of my ninety- three year-old dad that allows him to get up each day, find something to laugh about, make his doctors laugh, encourage his neighbors, and even through the pain of arthritis, count each day as a blessing.

I am encouraged to write, as my mother did, because she was birthed with poetry inside of her. I feel her spirit telling me to be creative, even from her grave. So, I will start sharing what I know.

I create every week. I prepare sermons. As of this writing, I have done it for forty-five years am sure that before this book is done, I will have to decide how candid to be and whether to use a pen name so that I can share some of the graphic horror stories of this pastor's experience. Yet there have been so many blessings.

Aunt Belle

Her real name was Isabelle Burrell Ware. When I started doing the family history, I learned that before she married Uncle Charlie Ware, who was deceased long before I was born, she had been married to a Moses Brandon—but not for long. She never mentioned that marriage. Neither did anyone else. The only way I knew was from US Census records. God knows that if she knew that I know this information, she would probably let out one of her blood-curdling screams that could wake up the dead in ten states and three foreign countries.

Aunt Belle was a comical person. She was very dramatic, as I mentioned earlier. One afternoon, Grandma had Aunt Belle over for dinner. Aunt Belle had caught the streetcar and then the bus to Grandma and Granddaddy's house. My mother and father had agreed to take her home after they got off from work. I know it was a Friday because Grandma and I had walked to the fish market to get fish for dinner. We are a Baptist family, but we ate fish on Friday. Grandma had fried plenty of fish, potatoes, and onions. She stewed tomatoes, cooked collard greens, and baked cornbread. She had also made iced tea. It was one delicious meal. I can taste it even now. But a problem occurred as we ate. A fly got into the dining room and began flying around the table. Aunt Belle waved it away. I was sitting next to her and waved it away. Granddaddy, who was sitting at the head of the table between Grandma and Aunt Belle, waved it away. Grandma was not going to have this uninvited guest ruin her dinner gathering. So she went to get the fly swatter.

Aunt Belle had a separate bowl beside her plate, in which she was neatly placing her fish bones. She was working on her second or third piece of fish. Grandma was attempting to swat the fly away from the table and the food. We knew she had it, but we were not sure where it landed. Thinking it had landed on the floor behind Aunt Belle and me, we continued to enjoy our peaceful meal. Aunt Belle started to comment on how good the fish was. All of a sudden, she stopped midsentence, looked down at the bowl of fish bones, and saw the "dearly departed" housefly. She dropped the fish bone she was holding, pointed at the bowl, and let out a blood-curdling scream.

Granddaddy looked up.

She said, "Fly!" and went back to screaming.

Granddaddy looked at me because I started laughing. For a moment, I thought he was going to scold me for being silly at the dinner table. But he gave a little smirk, shook his head, and kept on eating. Grandma jumped up, grabbed the bowl of fish bones from in front of Aunt Belle, and went to the kitchen with it so fast it would make your head spin. By this time, I was in tears. It was a laughter meltdown for me. Grandma came back with a clean bowl for a still-screaming Aunt Belle and threw two paper towels at me because I was laughing and crying so hard. Granddaddy just finished eating. Later, Grandma would laugh too.

Aunt Belle had a tender heart for the children in the family. I mentioned that for years she was "Santa's helper," making sure that her great-great nieces and nephews missed getting what was on our Christmas lists. Christmas dinner rotated each year from our house to Auntie and Uncle Sidney's to Grandma and Granddaddy's, but before we took Aunt Belle home, we always had to visit the other houses so she could see what all the children got for Christmas. Now I know why: she wanted to see the fruit of her labor and the joy it brought to our faces firsthand. But if she gave us some money and we tried to hug her, she would pretend she didn't want us to touch her. We'd just laugh it off. Some people seem grumpy on the surface but have soft hearts, while others seem sweet but are mean as snakes. You learn to know the difference.

Every year, we could expect that she was taking all of us to Hershey Park with her church, Canaan Baptist Church. Even if you were on punishment, she wouldn't take no for an answer. She'd tell our parents, "Postpone the punishment till next week or add a day. They are going with me! I have paid for the tickets." Sometimes, our parents would substitute a long, stern lecture for the remainder of the punishment, adding, "You better thank God you have an Aunt Belle!"

God, I still thank You for her and for all of the rest of them who shaped me. When my grandma Graham moved to DC to live with us, she and Aunt Belle became very close. Grandma Graham joined Canaan Baptist, and Aunt Belle paid so she could go on the trip too. She and Aunt Belle were great company for each other. Aunt Belle was very sad when Grandma Graham moved back to Youngstown, Ohio.

Third Sunday in July

Grandma Jackson was born and raised in Rectortown, Virginia, which is now virtually a suburb of DC but then was a two-and-a-half hour drive away on two-lane roads. She was born Rebecca Marsha Grant.

On the third Sunday in July, instead of going to Nineteenth Street Baptist Church, we would get up early in the morning and go to Mount Olive Baptist Church in Rectortown. Most of the church members were relatives, and many still are to this day. All those Grants are related to me! When my grandmother had her first heart attack, Freedmen's Hospital (the hospital in DC at which African Americans could be treated before desegregation) said only the spouse, siblings, children, and the nieces, nephews, and grandchildren above a certain age could visit. A large group of people showed up. The hospital began to ask questions. Grandma had several brothers and sisters still living at that time and a total of fifty-five nieces and nephews! Though Grandma only had two children, her two children had a lot of first cousins, aunts, and uncles. So for me, going to Rectortown was always fun because I had plenty *more* cousins—second, third, fourth, and fifth cousins!

We would go to church in the morning and hear preaching and singing that leaves an impression on me to this day. We'd eat dinner at a cousin's home (usually Cousin Malachi's) and then stop in to see Cousin Juanita before the adults went back to church for the evening worship. Many of us who could not get into the over crowded church would walk around outside and meet *more* cousins. After service, we would go up and down the road by the church seeing more relatives, at some point stopping at the home of Uncle Rob and Aunt Edmonia (Grandma's brother and sister-in-law). Then we would end up on Grant Mountain, where Cousin Foster and Cousin Virginia Grant lived, along with Cousin Frenchy, Cousin Bill Parker, Cousin Dorothy, Cousin Celestine, Cousin DePrice, Cousin Nathaniel, and Cousin Susie. I know I am forgetting some of my dad's first cousins who were up on that mountain, but they all had kids that we played with. The next day at home, I'd be swollen up like a balloon because I had childhood allergies to cats, dogs, weeds, grass, feathers, wool, and whatever else Dr. Owens could think of. But, oh, what fun it was to see chickens and hogs and dogs (I remember one dog named "Inky") and cats and to roll down the hill in Cousin Foster's grassy front yard and to play in the playhouse he had built. Of course, Grandma was always checking me for ticks on the way home.

Those Mount Olive worship services will forever be with me. They were so spirited and so moving. Something about them was calling out to me—it was calling me loudly. I was not sure what it was, but it would call out to me for days and weeks after the service. It would start calling to me the week before we would go each year. Years later, I would come to understand how the Holy Spirit was drawing me, reaching out to me by name, even when I was a young child.

In 2014, I spent the third Sunday in July at Mount Olive's evening service for the first time in many years. I had not been to the church since Cousin Foster's funeral. I drove up Atoka Road from US Route 50, past horse estates and a sign that says "Entering Historic Rectortown." I drove by houses that were built on land where great-aunts and great-uncles used to live and some of my third cousins were raised. Then I passed Cousin Juanita's house and Cousin Malachi's house and turned into the churchyard. The church had changed since my childhood, yet it was still the same. A large front porch with columns, a large narthex/foyer, an extended dining room, and an education wing had been added. There was still a large crowd of people.

Missing, however, were the saints of old whom I knew so well. They were now at rest in the arms of Jesus. Their children were now the seniors serving in the dining room as their parents, grandparents, aunts, and uncles once did. Here, I saw the great-nephews and great-nieces of my grandma Jackson—Grants by birth, serving with joy and pride as did their parents. As I was recognized and greeted, I once again felt that deep connection to family and heritage. I was welcomed like the prodigal son returning home.

I was introduced to the new pastor and spoke to the pastor emeritus, whom I had known since childhood. I have now known three generations of pastors at Mount Olive. I felt as though I had returned home. In a way, I had. It was a place that had played a big part in drawing me to Christ. I thought I was going to represent my father, who cannot travel long distances anymore because of arthritis. God had clearly set up this appointment for me. Church and worship was the way I remembered the worship experience. It had the same fervor and power. The pastor started a song that I had not heard in years but had learned from my uncle Louis in Youngstown, Ohio, at Mount Zion Baptist Church. He sang the first verse and looked to the choir for someone to take up the song, "This May Be the Last Time." None of them knew it. Sitting in the pulpit with the other preachers, I wailed a verse so the rafters of heaven would shake with praise. "May be the last time I see my friends…"

The church responded, "May be the last time, I don't know."

The next thing I knew, the pastor had handed the microphone over to me. I sang three more common-meter verses and led the chorus. I could feel the fine hairs on the back of my neck stand up as the Holy Spirit swept through the church. I felt as though I'd shrunk inside myself and was simply observing as the Holy Spirit took over the singing. Many times, I feel the presence of God in worship, especially when I am preaching. But on that third Sunday in July 2014, I felt that at any moment, we were all going to be raptured right from that worship service.

Once again, my cousins Earsaline, Jeffrey, Michael, and Eldon asked the question that their late parents used to ask my grandparents and my parents. "Are you coming to the house after service?"

Although Cousin Foster and Cousin Virginia are with Jesus, I knew right away that the after-church fellowship was *still* taking place at their home. Without a doubt, I was going.

I had not been on Grant Mountain in years. I had forgotten how peaceful it was there. The house was still the same. The only thing missing was the presence of Cousin Foster and Cousin Virginia. As Cousin Earsaline asked me to bless the food, I felt the presence of my grandparents and my cousins' parents and grandparents fill the room. As we all joined hands, I felt as though I heard the Lord say, "Wait till we do this in my father's house." I have had so many wonderful times in that house. So many memories. None was as anointed and moving for me as this homecoming day was.

I later walked Cousin Dorothy (Cousin Dot) back to her house, where Cousin Frenchy used to live. It was there I got a cell phone signal and had the privilege of making it possible for my father to talk with his first cousin, Dorothy. She is now close to ninety, and my dad is ninety. She said that conversation with him made her day. I could hear the excitement in both their voices. I could not wait to call my dad on the way back home to give him a full, detailed report of the day. Once again, the Lord used this Homecoming Sunday, the third Sunday in July, as a time to speak to me and show me the importance of family and the family connection. Yet He also showed me that there is a bigger connection—the people of God as a clan, *His* family.

The Graham Side of Family Village

Certain smells and sounds bring to mind more fond memories of my childhood. In DC, it was the smell and the sounds of streetcars and of Union Station because of my love for streetcars and trains. However, the strongest pull for me outside of DC are the smells, the sights, and the experiences I had in Youngstown, Ohio. This was the hometown of my mother. This was the place where Grandma Graham lived until she came to stay with us. It was the place she went back to until she went to be with Jesus. This is the place where her body now rests until

Jesus comes back for His church. It is the place I thought about going to live at one time because I like the way the people there worshipped!

My first trip there took place when I was an infant. I was five months old when my parents took me to Youngstown on the Baltimore and Ohio railroad for Thanksgiving. (That was my very first train ride.) There was a terrible snowstorm; three feet or more of snow fell. I was the only reason my parents did not get stranded there; the Red Cross got them to the B&O station because they had an infant, and it was considered an emergency situation. As my mother and father told the story, the train was so crowded that my father had to stand for a long time, and my mother sat in the ladies' lounge with me in a bassinet on the floor by what little heat was coming out of the register. I remember her saying that when we got home, I had pneumonia. My dad vowed never again to go up to Youngstown after October and before the "spring thaw." He kept his word.

One of my greatest joys was when my parents took vacations from their jobs and we went to visit Grandma Graham in Youngstown. For most African Americans, vacations were trips to visit family. During the years of segregation in this country, there were many places that people of color were not accepted and would be treated cruelly or even killed just because of the color of their skin. This was particularly noticeable in the South. As African Americans, we learned which places were safe to stop to use a restroom, which towns and stretches of highway to avoid if possible, which restaurants we could patronize, and which gas stations would not try to cheat us out of our money. In most cases, everyone, whether traveling north or south, topped off the gas tank before the trip, stayed up and cooked food the day before, packed picnic baskets and thermos jugs of water and other beverages, and carried plenty of snacks for the trip. This way, we did not have to take any chances on suffering an embarrassment that could ruin the trip. My parents and the rest of my family did their best to shelter us kids from the ugliness and sickness of our society. They made preparing for the trip a fun adventure. I would be so excited about going to see my grandma Graham, Aunt Katie, Uncle Morris, Donald, Nancy, Kenny, and Aunt Cinnie, who married Uncle Louis when I was six. Then there is my mother's youngest brother, Uncle Glenn, who is the last of his siblings left. It was hard for me to believe that my mother had a brother who was only twelve years older than I was. He was only two years older than my cousin, Vernon, was. Granddaddy Jackson had an uncle Benny—Nana and Aunt Belle's youngest brother—who was only five years older than my grandfather was. I would not understand those things until I was older and learned about "late-in-life babies."

Grandma Graham

I loved going to visit Grandma Mary S. Graham. I always thought she was the tallest woman in the world. She was five foot eleven and a half. For a woman, that was tall. She was born in Autauga County, Alabama. She and Granddaddy Graham had moved to Youngstown from Prattville, Alabama, with their three children, Marzett (Uncle Zetty), Morris, and Cynthia (Aunt Cinnie) before my mother was born. During the Great Depression, Granddaddy Graham went to Dayton, Ohio, to find work. Grandma stayed in Youngstown with the three children. Granddaddy Graham eventually became a cement finisher in Dayton, but the family home remained in Youngstown.

On the Graham side of the family, Grandma Graham was the undisputed matriarch for her entire life. She carried herself in a way that always commanded respect from everyone with whom she came in contact. Her youngest child (my uncle Glenn) gave her the nickname "Prez," short for President. It made Grandma blush. The rest of my uncles and my mother thought it was so cute that the name stuck. As I was talking with my uncle Glenn about how the name Prez came to be, he shared with me that when he wanted something or wanted permission to do something, using this affectionate term was a way of melting his mother's heart. Several things stand out about Grandma Graham, other than her height. She was soft-spoken and resourceful. She held deep convictions about her walk with the Lord and made no apologies for it. As far back as I can remember, she read her Bible daily. You could see her praying anytime during the day, whenever she felt the need.

We have been Baptist on both sides of my family as far back as I can remember. For us, it was not just about "going to church." Grandma Graham was truly saved. She was not a jumper or a shouter, but you could tell when the Holy Spirit had moved her during a worship service. She would pat her knee, tap her foot, and sometimes shed tears through a smile. She listened intently to sermons and later went over the scripture. Sometimes she wrote little notes about the sermon she'd heard or the scripture verse she'd read and stuck them in her Bible. Only a few times did I ever see her have a big, emotional "outpouring of the Spirit." None was in a church setting.

Once was at the home of Uncle Morris and Aunt Katie. I don't remember what was going on. I was extremely young. Grandma grabbed a dining room chair, got down on her knees, and started praying and crying with a handkerchief in her hand. I remember walking up to the chair and standing there, looking at her. I must have been a toddler because my eyes were at the level of the chair's armrest. Grandma was praying hard and pounding that chair. Everyone else got quiet. The only words I remember hearing were, "God, You heard my prayer! Thank You, Jesus!" Whatever it was, Grandma had gotten her answer.

Another time, she was scrubbing the kitchen floor of her home. She was obviously praying while she was scrubbing the floor on her hands and knees. For some reason, no one was there but Grandma and me. I was in her front room, sitting on the floor, playing with some toys I had brought from home. I must have been three or four years old. I heard Grandma yell out praise to God.

I went to her and touched her shoulder. "What's wrong, Grandma?" I asked.

"Leave me alone, baby, Grandma is all right!" she said, smiling through tears. "I was just talking with Jesus."

She had splashed water out of her scrub bucket, and the scrub brush was halfway across the kitchen, but there she was, in the middle of the kitchen floor, which she had consecrated into a tabernacle of God's presence.

The other time that left an impression on me happened when I was three years old. My parents had taught me to recite the twenty-third psalm. We had worked on it for days and weeks, constantly going over it. (Yes, I was three years old and did not know how to read.) The day that I recited it in front of the Nineteenth Street Baptist Church, my parents and grandparents were so proud of me.

The next evening, Grandma Graham came to visit us from Youngstown on the B&O Railroad. When we got her back to our apartment, my father had me recite the psalm as I had done at church the day before. When I finished reciting, Grandma grabbed me in her arms and yelled, "Praise God! Betty, Walter, this baby is going to be my preacher!" Tears rolled down her face, and she held me tightly while rocking back and forth. Though this incident happened sixty-one years ago, I remember it vividly—as clearly as if it happened just yesterday. I have had flashbacks of that moment at milestones and challenges in my ministry. Grandma Graham saw in the Spirit things that would happen in my life years later. She lived to see the beginnings of them.

Grandma Graham was a prayer warrior and one who spent time in God's word. Several times a day, she read her Bible. I remember her routine. She got up each day and went to one special spot where she would pray. When she was in Youngstown, Ohio, I remember seeing her sit on the porch at 622½ Himrod Avenue, which overlooked the place where Himrod, Wilson, and Penn avenues met Federal Street, across from the New York Central Train Station. She sometimes sat out there, reading her Bible and praying. Other times, she would sit in her front room and pray. I always knew that Grandma's prayers worked when no one else's would. I felt she had a connection with God that was different. As I think about it now, I never asked my grandmother when and how she came to know Christ. I wish I had.

I just know from her witness, life, and testimony that one day Christ became very real for her. He was the center of her life and the reason for her existence. Everything she did and the way she related to her family, church, and people in general was due to her relationship with Christ. Even before I fully understood what it meant to be saved and to have a relationship with Christ, I knew that to offend or disrespect Grandma was to offend God, because she belonged to *Him*.

Sitting on Grandma Graham's front porch over the Pittsburgh Paint store was a peaceful thing for me. As I write this, I can once again see, hear, and smell Youngstown of the mid-1950s. I can hear the vanishing steam-engine whistles and the first-generation diesels bringing trains in and out of the New York Central Station. I can hear the humming traction motors of trolley buses making their way up and down Himrod and Wilson avenues and Federal Street. I can hear the whistles of steel mills at the shift changes, see the glowing molten steel being poured at a distance, and smell the distinct pungent odor of the smoke from the steel mill stacks. To me, these are sweet sounds and smells associated with a place I loved and people I loved who loved me, particularly Grandma Graham.

She loved not only me. She made all of her children and grandchildren feel special. She treated her sons-in-law and daughters-in-law as though they were her own children. She enjoyed family functions. Whether it was watching grandchildren play while sitting on the front porch at Uncle Morris and Aunt Katie's, sitting at a picnic area at an amusement park—Idora Park in Youngstown or Hershey Park in Pennsylvania—or sitting on a beach like Sandy Point or Fort Smallwood, she enjoyed family times. She would sometimes insist that we grandkids have a competition. Two times, in particular, stand out.

We had a family outing to the beach at Fort Smallwood State Park in Maryland, opposite Sparrows Point, I believe while Uncle Morris, Aunt Katie, Donald, Nancy, and Kenny were visiting during their vacation. With us were Uncle Zetty, Aunt Mable, and Cousin Bobby. After swimming and eating, Grandma Graham decided that she wanted to see her grandchildren have a footrace on the sand. A group of us ran once, and our parents and Grandma sat there laughing and cheer-ing. Grandma decided we needed to run again, and this time, she was going to run too. We children thought that was funny and wonderful that Grandma was going to run. Our parents were on the sidelines, saying, "Oh, Mother. No!" However, Grandma had the final say.

We all lined up to run—Donald, Nancy, Kenny, Cynthia, Bobby, Grandma (in a dress), and me. The race started. My cousins and my sister were all running. Grandma was running beside me, but she lost her footing in the loose sand, and down she went, laughing. My parents, aunts, and uncles hopped to their feet in shock, competing in the third race of the day—the one I'll call "the faster-than-a-New-York-minute sprint"—as they ran over to Grandma. She was lying in the sand and laughing uncontrollably, and I was trying to help her to her feet. She had sand everywhere, even in her dentures.

I never saw who won the grandchildren's second race. The adults' race to Grandma was an undisputed tie. I think the adults moved as a unit—one in the spirit. Grandma, still laughing, said to them, "I didn't know you all could move that fast." Thank God, she was not hurt at all. Her children said, "No more races for you, Mother!" That was the one time that she listened when her children told her what to do. She did not dispute them.

The next week, there was a trip to another beach. This time, we went to Sandy Point State Park on the Chesapeake Bay. This must have been the year that the beaches were integrated. Otherwise, we only would have been able to go to Sparrows Beach or Carr's Beach. Of course, after swimming and eating, Grandma Graham insisted again that her grandchildren have a footrace. Our parents quickly told Grandma she was not running. Grandma said this race was go-ing to be different. This time, there would be a boys' race and then a girls' race. Then the winners of each would race each other.

Let me give you a sidebar comment about my family. We are a family of great cooks with deep southern roots on both sides of the family. Homemade barbecue sauce, potato salad, spareribs, ham-burgers, and hot dogs were picnic staples, and *baked beans* were always served at our summer family gatherings. They were always delicious, and I remember this rhyme from childhood:

> Beans, beans good for your heart,
> The more you eat, the more you fart.
> The more you fart, the better you feel.
> So eat those beans at every meal.

This race would be the very last one that Grandma would organize, but it would be most memorable. We, her grandchildren, would laugh about it for years. There were four grandson contestants and two granddaughter contestants. The boys ran first. In order of age, it was Donald, me, Kenny, and Bobby. Donald won the boys' race, being oldest and tallest, though we all ran extremely hard the distance of a half a football field and back. That race went off without a hitch.

Then Grandma called for her two granddaughters to take their marks. Nancy and Cynthia were both wearing what were called pedal-pusher pants. Grandma yelled, "Go!" Those two young girls took off running like a pair of Thoroughbred horses at the Kentucky Derby. Then something happened that again took the focus off the race.

For a split second, everyone in the entire picnic area looked up. The runners must have had a surge of speed, but the sound we heard from half a football field away sounded like a tractor-trailer horn blowing. In fact, it was the sound of one of the runners having a flagellant moment. Yes, you heard me! One of them had passed gas very loudly while running. Neither girl lost her stride. To this day, we do not know who it was. It does not matter. What does matter is that it was loud, and it echoed and reverberated from a great distance. Grandma laughed so hard that she shook all over. People in the picnic areas on either side of us were laughing. Ten minutes later, we were still trying to pull ourselves together. I don't know who won the race, other than the "mighty rushing wind" that was not the Holy Spirit.

Grandma never called for another race after that. I don't think any of us wanted to chance what would happen at another one of her footraces. Spending time with my Graham cousins was as much fun as spending time with my cousins on the Jackson side of the family. In Youngstown, we would have cookouts in the backyard of Uncle Morris, Aunt Katie, Donald, Nancy, and Kenny. Grandma liked watching us eat and having a good time. Sometimes, in a serious tone, she would ask someone to go into the house and get her a calendar. When you asked her why, she would respond, "So I can see when Walter and Kenny are going to be full." This would prompt an outburst of laughter.

Once, Uncle Zetty organized a fishing trip. We got up at 2:00 a.m.; drove to Lewis, Delaware; boarded a chartered boat; and went deep-sea fishing. I don't think any of us had seen the Atlantic Ocean before—or any ocean, for that matter. We went so far out into the ocean that I asked if we were still in the United States. As we traveled out to the spot where we would drop anchor and fish, Uncle Zetty looked up from preparing the clam bait and saw a whale going the opposite direction. None of us had ever seen anything so big. It was bigger than our boat. I remember watching the whale leap out of the water, into the air, and then dive down to the water again. Every time it jumped up, Aunt Katie screamed, covered her mouth, and hollered, "Oh, look at it! Look at it!" Then she screamed again. Aunt Katie was scared. We kids would just laugh.

We caught several ice chests full of ling, bass, and sea robins which we threw back. To this day, I still love deep-sea fishing, even though I don't get to do it often.

One evening that week, we all packed into Uncle Morris's Ford station wagon for a trip to the Hot Shop Drive-in Restaurant. You ordered your food from your car over a radio speaker. The server would bring it out and hook the tray onto a stand by the driver's window.

Station wagons were the minivans of today. Packed into this station wagon were Daddy, Momma, Grandma Graham, Uncle Morris, Aunt Katie, Uncle Zetty, Aunt Mable, Donald, Nancy, Kenny, Bobby, my sister Cynthia, and me. We must have looked like a black version of the Beverly Hillbillies crammed into that station wagon as we rolled into the restaurant at Thirteenth and Rhode Island Avenue NE that evening. By the time we finished ordering Mighty Mos, fish sandwiches, french fries, onion rings, Cokes and orange freezes (I had two Mighty Mos, two orders of onion rings, and two orange freezes), the manager walked out to see if there really was a customer ordering all that food. Of course, we had a good laugh at that. It took four servers to bring the food out. People in other cars were really looking hard. They could not believe what they were seeing, with all those people and all that food. I ate so much I could barely breathe.

We used to love going to the wharf in DC and getting several bushels of crabs when my Youngstown family would visit. Auntie and Uncle Sidney would also come over, bringing DeLyse, Karen, and Ora Marie, so both sides of my family would be there together, having a crab feast. We'd cover the table with newspaper and dump the crabs on the table. We would spend hours eating crabs. Aunt Katie always broke out in a fine rash all over her body. She thought she was allergic to DC water. Years later, we realized that she was allergic to eating crabs.

One year, we visited Youngstown during the Fourth of July celebration. Not realizing that fireworks were not legal in Youngstown, we brought the fireworks we had purchased legally in DC. No one said a word to us about legality. After dark, Uncle Morris said, "We'll shoot those off back here, behind the house."

It didn't register with us that none of the neighbors was shooting off fireworks. We stayed in the backyard with our sparklers, which didn't make noise. As we started shooting off the Roman candles and other things that went up in the air, I noticed neighborhood kids gathering in the yard next door. Some adults were there also. My uncle invited some of my cousins' friends to come and sit and watch, telling them that they had to be kind of quiet. The adults watching from the back porches on either side were also quiet. Before we were finished, three yards were full of children watching our fireworks. After it was over, the kids disappeared as quickly as they had appeared.

My uncle and my dad shoveled the debris into the barrel they used for burning things. I heard Uncle Morris say, "Walter, fireworks are illegal in Youngstown."

My dad's shocked response was, *"Do what?"*

My uncle said, "But the children had a good time." Then I understood why the kids were so quiet and none had his or her own fireworks. This was a special treat for the entire neighborhood.

Uncle Morris threw some wood into the barrel and started a fire (which was legal). Then, if anyone were to stop and ask questions, we were just having a late-evening, 1958-version of a fire pit. That was the most daring thing I ever saw the adults in my family do. The fireworks never went to Youngstown again, but I doubt any of the kids on West Scott Street ever forgot the treat that my dad innocently brought from Washington, DC, that summer. Grandma had been inside reading her Bible and praying that no one would get hurt or get in trouble. I saw a side of Uncle Morris that I had never seen before—he wanted all of the children to have a great time and a new experience, even at the risk of paying a hefty fine.

It was exciting for me to attend the Mount Zion Baptist Church in Youngstown. My grandmother had been a member since she had moved from Prattville, Alabama, in the early 1920s. To this day, the church sits on the hill on Wilson Avenue. It has been rebuilt and is no longer the gray, wood-frame structure that I remember. When they were constructing the new church on the site, it was exciting to see it going up. The worship services were what impressed me, even as a child. This was Grandma Graham's church, in my mind. This was where she raised my mother, my aunt Cinnie, and my uncles Marzett, Morris, and Glenn. (Had Leo not died as an infant before my mother was born, he would have been raised there, too.) My family had roots there.

Most of the church members, I would later realize, had migrated to Youngstown from places in the Deep South to find work and to escape the harsh conditions of racism and segregation, which was at least more subtle in the North. They brought with them the common-meter style of singing, the lively foot tapping, and the double-time clapping with a fervor of spirit that would make the hairs on the back of your neck stand up three blocks away. The choir didn't sing behind a pipe organ, as did the choir at Nineteenth Street Baptist in DC. The choir sang behind a Hammond B3 with a Leslie speaker and an upright piano. They sang many of the same hymns but with a different beat. Those common-meter hymns continue to hold my soul and spirit captive to this day. They were so much like the ones sung at Mount Olive Baptist in Rectortown.

Both of my grandmothers came from spirited churches. That is the spirit that captivated me. It kept drawing me and calling me. "What is this message?" I would ask myself. "I *know* it is for me that it is calling!"

Rev. W. A. Clark was the pastor of Mount Zion. He had a style of preaching unlike what I heard at Nineteenth Street. He would start off like Reverend Moore did, but near the middle or toward the end of the sermon, he would begin to move around the pulpit a little more. His hand gestures would become more pronounced. His voice would take on a quality of singing or chanting, and the people would start answering. The piano and organ would sometimes get on the same pitch and follow him too. Before the sermon was over, people would be on their feet. Someone would have begun to shout. The ushers and nurse would have to attend someone with one of those funeral-home fans and or smelling salts. Then Reverend Clark would extend the invitation to Christ, and someone would come forward. That was *church!* (Pronounced "chuch.")

Grandma Graham was extremely active in the church—not because it was something to do but because she was committed to Christ. She lived her faith. It was not just talk or a "Sunday performance." She was not, as a friend of mine calls it, "fabulous fake." She was genuine in her relationship with Christ. If you accompanied her to the hospital to visit someone, it would be nothing to lose her because she had walked into another room and struck up a conversation. She would be praying with a total stranger. If she happened to go back to the hospital while that stranger was still a patient, she'd be invited in again. Her prayer life is still an inspiration to me. With the spiritual maturity I have now, I often wish that my grandmothers and Granddaddy Jackson were still here with me today. Oh, the things I would love to share with them.

My Mother's Brothers

My mother had four brothers. In the order of their birth, they were Uncle Marzett, Uncle Morris, Uncle Leo (who died as an infant), and the youngest and only surviving sibling, Uncle Glenn. The Grahams are tall. To me, the uncles were giants of men. They stood tall, proud, polished, and distinguished, and they had very calm personalities. They, like my father, were gentlemen. They were gentlemen whom people respected and treated with respect. They shared an unwritten standard of excellence in attire, poise, and work ethic. From a very young age, I saw all of these things in all my uncles, my father, and my grandfathers. They always looked professional to me in whatever they did because of how they carried themselves. I thank them for the positive examples I saw in them.

My uncles were self-taught but accomplished musicians. Each of them could play several instruments or had some general knowledge of them. Uncle Zetty played mostly electric guitar. Uncle Morris played piano, organ, and saxophone. Uncle Glenn played vibraharp. A group he sang with produced an album called the *Moderns Go to College* around 1958. He sang the lead on a song called "Spring Came Along." Uncle Zetty and Uncle Morris had played in bands and in nightclubs during the big band era. They were all, in my opinion, great musicians.

As Uncle Glenn later summed it up at my cousin Kenny's (Kenneth Graham) funeral years later, "Music and spirituality has played a major role in our family as far back as any of us can remember."

I remember watching my uncles play music together in Uncle Morris and Aunt Katie's living room until the early morning once. I don't know when they stopped because I fell asleep. I don't know who put me in bed at their house. When I woke up, it was morning, the jam session was over, and everybody was just waking up for breakfast, laughing, joking, and having fun just being family. Man, that felt good!

Years later, as a school librarian, I thought of my uncles when I read the novel *Bud Not Buddy* by Christopher Paul Curtis. He mentions the character "Herman E. Calloway" and his band, who would have been contemporaries of the author's grandfather in real life. They also lived in the Midwest and played jazz. Christopher Paul Curtis, by the way, is one of my favorite authors. I saw an interview with him when I was teaching this past year and was very impressed with him. His family story reminds me of mine.

Watching Uncle Morris on the piano and organ made me want to play both. I took piano lessons for a short time—long enough to learn the notes and the proper fingering. I wanted to learn to play gospel music as they played at Mount Zion, but my piano teacher wanted me to play classical music because I had a knack for piano and learned quickly. I realized that I was picking up the patterns in the music and that I had an ear for it. However, I didn't like classical music. I didn't want to play it. We sang classical anthems at Nineteenth Street Baptist. Founded in 1839, it is the oldest African-American Baptist church in Washington, DC. Among the congregants, my family is one of the oldest, going back eight generations now. The church has had some very famous members, one being Charles Drew. The original location was only three blocks from the White House.

Growing up with music, singing in choirs, having uncles who played (Uncle Glenn) and sang in the men's chorus at Mount Zion (Uncle Louis, married to Aunt Cinnie), plus two grandfathers, a father, a mother, a sister, an Auntie (my father's sister), and DC cousins who sang in choirs, I knew how to find my tenor, baritone, or bass line and sing my part. I just wanted to play gospel, period! My piano teacher did not want me to learn it. So I quit taking lessons and taught myself what I wanted to know. I also learned how to play the Hammond B3. Now I wish I had stuck with the lessons. There would be so much more I could do with gospel music now.

On trips to Youngstown, my parents, my sister, and I would sing hymns for the last half hour or so of the trip. Each of us knew our parts of the songs. Since we all had wide ranges, we would adjust the key, and Momma would sing the soprano part; Cynthia, the alto; Daddy, the baritone or bass part; and I would sing the tenor part. Sometimes, it would just be Momma and Daddy singing duets.

So, my family gave me a music legacy along with everything else. For the most part, the instrumental music came from the Graham side of the family, and the vocal part came from the Jackson side, with a couple of exceptions to the rule. The strong work ethic was ever present in both the Graham and Jackson clans—my family. *My royalty!*

Uncle Louis and Aunt Cinnie

My mother had one sister, who was six years older than she was. Aunt Cinnie's name was actually Cynthia Graham, but we always called her Aunt Cinnie.

My earliest memory of her was looking at her through the window of a hospital, where she was being treated for tuberculosis. When we went to Youngstown to visit Grandma, we would go to see Aunt Cinnie at the hospital they referred to as "the San." I remember that on the grounds of this place, there were apple trees. I remember picking apples there once and Grandma making them into a couple of her famous apple cobblers. Her apple and peach cobblers and turnovers were the best I've ever eaten. I was blessed to have two grandmothers, a mother, and three aunts who were excellent cooks.

I learned later from testimony that Aunt Cinnie gave when teaching Sunday school, Bible studies, and workshops, that while she was hospitalized for a number of years with tuberculosis, she got rather down one time. She had a vision or a dream that she was in a place where many people were standing around, looking into a light where there was the figure of a man. She asked people who the man was, and they said He was Jesus.

She said, "Well, let's go through the fog and talk to him."

The others said, "We can't get through that fog."

She said, "Yes, we can! He's just on the other side. Don't you see?" She went through the fog alone. No one else would go.

The Lord said to her, "Cynthia, what will you have me to do?"

She said, "Lord, restore my health."

The Lord told her to teach His people. As I remember her testimony, she began to teach a Bible study while in the hospital for the women in the ward. It was so powerful that the doctors instructed the nurses that they were not to be disturbed during the Bible study.

The doctors had decided to try a new treatment for her condition. She was to lie on her back with her feet elevated higher than her head to drain the fluid from her lungs. While she lay there, the other women, who could move about, would gather around her bed for Bible study.

Aunt Cinnie was in the hospital longer than most of the women were. I remember her saying that when the women were discharged, the relationships they had developed with Christ prepared them to go home to be with their families or to go home to be with the Lord. Aunt Cinnie was a Bible teacher for the rest of her life.

Later in life, she attended college, as did Uncle Glenn, and got a bachelor's degree in Christian education. She was my motivation to do graduate studies in theology. Uncle Glenn went on to get a master's degree.

Grandma Graham only finished the eighth grade, but her father, my great-grandfather, was one of her teachers in school, and my great-aunt Annie would later become a principal.

Uncle Louis met Aunt Cinnie at church. As I began writing this book, my uncle Glenn helped me to connect many of the dots in this section of the story. Some pieces of the story are very moving.

Uncle Louis and Uncle Glenn sang in the Mount Zion Male Chorus. Uncle Glenn was the vessel that God used to open the doorway for Uncle Louis to come into the family and forge a place in our lives that was not only powerful but also powerfully positive.

Louis Riggins would take my uncle Glenn home from male chorus rehearsal. On one of those occasions, Aunt Cinnie was at home. Though Louis Riggins had seen Aunt Cinnie at church, he had not realized that she was Uncle Glenn's sister. Uncle Glenn formally introduced him to Aunt Cinnie, and then, as Uncle Glenn put it, Uncle Louis was on his own.

I remember Uncle Louis and Aunt Cinnie's wedding very well. I was six, and my sister, Cynthia, who was named after Aunt Cinnie, was two. Uncle Glenn was the soloist at Uncle Louis and Aunt Cinnie's wedding. From that point on, Louis Riggins was Uncle Louis.

Their home was like a second home for me. When I would visit them, my bedroom was in the attic, which I called "my apartment." I loved spending a great portion of my summer with them. I have a wonderful father, but Uncle Louis was my "summer dad" and the one who witnessed to me, sharing with me my now favorite scripture, John 14:1–6. He had me read it once and assist him with devotions as if I were a junior deacon during an afternoon worship service at Mount Zion. I shall never forget that experience and the witness he was to me. Most of the old-time common-meter gospel songs I know I learned either from Uncle Louis or at worship services at Mount Zion or at Mount Olive in Rectortown. They were songs like "Hide Me in the Rock," "I Know I've Been Changed," "You Can't Make Me Doubt Him," and "If Anybody Ask You Who I Am." The last one I learned from him before his death was "The Blood Done Signed My Name," which he sang at my church when Aunt Cinnie was our Women's Day speaker the year before his passing. There was a Bible in every room in their home, and they were not decorations. They were read and studied.

Uncle Glenn called him "Pops" because he was a father figure to him.

Uncle Louis was a true armor bearer for the pastor and a preacher/pastor encourager. He was to a preacher like a coach is to a prize-fighter. He knew just what to say at just the right moment for just the right situation to pick up your spirits or make you feel as though you could take on the world for the cause of Christ. He had no college education, but his wisdom and understanding of God's word was amazing. Uncle Louis would talk, and I would hang on every word, soaking them in like a sponge. Even the things that I did not fully understand then, I would later make sense of as I grew in the Lord. I am thankful for those summers that I spent with him and Aunt Cinnie in Youngstown. It was as though my parents had deliberately sent me there to reinforce the things that they had spent so much time teaching me with a slightly different technique. When I went into the ministry, we would spend hours discussing scripture and a sermon he had heard or one I had preached. I can almost hear him now. "Walter, listen; this is how I see this passage or that passage. What do you get out of it?"

My Parents, and My Sister

It seems that the great meeting place in my family—and the place where romances began—was church. My grandparents, Aunt Cinnie and Uncle Louis, and my parents all met at church.

When my mother (then Betty Louise Graham) graduated from high school, she went to Washington, DC, and was hired as a federal employee. She stayed with her brother, Uncle Zetty, who was a DC police officer at that time. She wanted to fulfill the requirement of the Baptist covenant that says, "When you remove from this place you will unite with some other church where we can carry out the spirit of this covenant and the principles of God's word." That meant that she was going to "unite with another church of the same faith and order." So, on her first Sunday in DC, that is what she did. She was told about one church, the Nineteenth Street Baptist Church. It is the oldest African American Baptist church in Washington, DC, established in 1839. My family is one of the oldest in the church, now going back eight generations. My mother joined on that very first Sunday and soon joined the choir, where she met my father, Walter A. Jackson Jr.

They were married on July 12, 1947, at my grandparent's house. The reception was at Uncle Zetty's house, across the Potomac River in Virginia.

Three years later, I came along; and four years after that, my sister Cynthia came along. I guess Cynthia and I were like most brother-and-sister duos. We had our squabbles as kids. Some of them probably worried our parents big time. The only part of my sister's story I will tell you, out of respect and love for her, is the turning point in our relationship that forever validated our bond and love. It happened after the tragic death of our cousin, Vernon, who was murdered in Southeast Washington at the age of twenty-eight.

Cynthia was sent to pick me up at Union Station, as I had taken the train home from college a few days before the Thanksgiving break to be with our family. We had never experienced anything like this. We had experienced Nana's death in 1966, but she was ninety-three and had been failing with dementia. That was different. Vernon was our cousin! He was only eight years older than I was and twelve years older than Cynthia was! Other families experienced this stuff, not *ours*! Auntie had lost her firstborn child! DeLyse, Karen, and Ora Marie had lost their big brother! This was wrong. What if this had been *me*? What if this had been *my only sibling, my sister*?

As I write this, I am reliving the moment. I got off the train with tears in my eyes and saw my sister standing on the concourse of Union Station. She stood there looking at me as I walked up to her. My thoughts were, "Oh, thank God! I still have you!" Without saying a word, I dropped my bags, and we fell into each other's arms and wept bitterly for what seemed like an eternity. Not a word was spoken. I don't remember a word we said to each other on the trip to our grandparents' house, where the whole family had gathered.

From that moment on, Cynthia and I have been tighter than thieves. We can even sense each other in the spirit. I can think of her, and she will call; or she can think of me, and I will call her. It is almost as though we have twin spirits. I was blessed to lead her to the Lord after praying for her for seven years. It was also an honor to perform her wedding to her late husband, Rev. Aubrey Swann, in my home and to preach her ordination sermon when she was ordained a minister.

Raised in the Family Village

In our family, grandparents, aunts, and uncles—as well as your parents—had the right to correct you. The entire family held stakes in our lives. They wanted the very best for us. I remember hearing, "I don't want these children to have to go through what we had to go through." It was not always about being spanked when we got out of hand. It was mostly about being exposed to educational experiences, places, and events. They took us to cultural events that many people would consider too old for children. We were taken to concerts at the Daughters of the American Revolution Constitution Hall after integration and taught how to dress up to go to places like that. We were taken to formal banquets at hotels and taught how to eat at a formal table setting. We were taught that if you don't know what to do, you observe the head table. (I have been to some events and wanted to scream because the people at the head table didn't do it right.)

Things were not as they are today. If Grandma or Granddaddy reprimanded you, my parents would say, "Don't come crying to me. You better be glad they are older now and don't hit as hard." If some adult in the neighborhood or church told your family about how you were acting in public out of their sight, you got in trouble for embarrassing the family. Jacksons were expected to act a certain way everywhere. To borrow my dad's phrase, "You don't act like little heathens!"

You learned the family warning signals. There were the finger snaps. Those, you got if the adult was on the telephone and you were starting to act out. If Grandma Jackson was on the phone and you were misbehaving, she would reach up to her shoulder and grab the dish towel that seemed to stay there all day.

Then there were the church warnings. My sister, my cousins, and I sat with Grandma in the balcony on the Pennsylvania Avenue side of the old Nineteenth Street Baptist Church, at a right angle to the choir, where Granddaddy and Daddy sang baritone in the back row by the pipe organ, and Auntie and Momma sang alto in the front row. Grandma seated herself behind us on the second of three rows in the section of the balcony known as "the Jackson pews"; that's just where we sat. That way, Grandma could reach over and tap you on the shoulder if you got out of hand. She didn't weigh but ninety pounds, as I mentioned earlier, but she was strong. She was not above reaching over the pew and snatching you back to sit next to her. That ended whatever behavior you were exhibiting.

When you got home from church, nothing would be said—until you asked for permission to do something. Then your parents would ask, "Why did Grandma have to move you?" When you gave the answer, your parents would respond, "Well, I guess you won't be watching Walt Disney tonight, since you don't know how to act in church. Is that right?"

Grandma was a deaconess, so if she was down on the main floor on Communion Sunday helping with baptism and Communion, "the look" from the choir kept us in check. Any one of four people could give us the look—Granddaddy, Daddy, Auntie, or Momma. When the look was given, whoever saw it first would elbow the next sibling or cousin until we all made eye contact with our parents and grandfather in the choir. That was the *only* warning we would get. If Grandma looked up from her deaconess duties and they saw her look our way, there was no warning. Someone was in deep trouble. If you did not heed the warning, or if Grandma looked up from the main floor, one of your parents would leave the choir, step into the vestibule off the balcony, and point to the offending child. It didn't matter if you were his or her child or a niece or nephew. (Granddaddy was never the one to leave his spot next to the organ. He would delegate someone to go tend to his grandchildren.) The offending child would be invited into the vestibule, and the door would be closed for a brief moment. You would hear a couple of muffled popping sounds as the "right hand of fellowship" connected with the place upon which one sits.

The adult would send the child back in after whispering, "I dare you to make one sound, or I will take you downstairs and give you something to cry for."

You would go back in and take a seat, tears rolling down your face, but not a sound would come out of your mouth to disrupt the service. After church, Grandma would say, "If you do that next Sunday, I'll knock you for a row of ash cans!" That always gave me a visual image of her hitting one of us with the dish towel, sending us spinning down an alley, knocking over cans full of ashes from people's coal furnaces.

Everybody on the main floor knew the Jackson children would not get too far out of hand. They would look up, see us, and know what just had happened. They all said we were well trained, and we were. We knew well that rule about behaving at church.

Momma and Daddy did the best they could by us. They set good examples by having a good work ethic. My parents, Auntie, Uncle Sidney, Aunt Belle, Aunt Ethel, and my grandparents all either worked or had worked for the federal government. I thought they kept it running. To me, they *were* the government.

Momma had a saying, "A job worth doing is worth doing well," which stayed with me long after her passing. Once, when Cynthia and I were doing our Saturday chores, we did not do the vacuuming and dusting to Momma's satisfaction. I believe this is the day I really learned to pray. Momma's tone of voice showed that she clearly was not pleased with our work. She snatched the dust rag out of Cynthia's hand and proceeded to bend down to show us how she wanted us to dust the legs of the furniture. Cynthia drew back her foot, pretending to kick Momma in the rear! I must have had a look of sheer horror on my face as Momma looked back while Cynthia's foot was in midair. Several thoughts ran through my head in that instant:

1. Daddy is going to come home from work and find two dead children on the living room floor and a wife in handcuffs.
2. Cynthia was going to have a broken leg, and I would be covered in Pledge, having been used as the dust rag.
3. Cynthia and I would be adults before our friends would see us again because we would be punished for so long.

In that instant, I remember praying, *"Please God, don't let her kill us!"* I must have looked so scared, so serious, and so full of trauma that when Momma looked up, all she did was laugh. I almost fainted!

Then Momma said, "I think we've done enough work today." We ended up having one of our many Saturday discussions. Cynthia and I have often laughed about that incident.

Momma was a complex person. She was very private, in a way, but she was also very creative. She would have been a great schoolteacher. She was a writer-editor in the government before she retired. She also wrote poetry. I hope to get it republished so that a larger audience can see her genius and create a legacy for the great-grandchildren she did not live to see. I feel even now her motivation to continue in this writing. I can hear her coaching words, "Tell 'em what you are going to tell 'em. Tell 'em. Then tell 'em that you told 'em." I don't know how many times I heard that sentence as I was growing up and while I was writing my first few sermons. Even now when I prepare sermons, I think of that. When I was in the classroom preparing lessons for students, I would think of that. Those simple words describe the basics of an effective lesson or sermon.

Daddy was a hard worker. He and Momma made many sacrifices for Cynthia and me. I am so truly grateful. These are the two who sat up with me all night when, at seven years old, I was on the verge of rheumatic fever and was having convulsions. I remember seeing the worry in their eyes, even though I was hallucinating. I didn't do a lot of talking as I was growing up, but I did a lot of watching and listening. I watched Daddy work—and work hard. I listened to him sing in church with feeling. I watched Momma and him, as deaconess and deacon, serve Communion to the sick and to shut-ins. I watched them do the best they knew to do in parenting Cynthia and me. (I can say that *now*.)

Even when I was forty-five, and they were in their sixties, when the doctor thought I was having a heart attack, they drove to West Virginia from DC to see for themselves that I was OK. They were not just going to take my word. They wanted to see me for themselves. I realized then that although I was grown, I was still their child and always would be. Nothing would ever change that. They drove for an hour and a half just to see me for themselves. They were there for only about thirty minutes, long enough to see that I was truly OK, and it was as I said—only a reaction to the blood pressure medicine. When they left, I turned my face to the window and watched them get into the car. I prayed as they drove off, and I cried. I was grown! I was and am a pastor! However, I was and am *still* their child.

There is no authoritative book on parenthood other than the model God gives of how He relates to those who love Him. I thank God that Walter A. Jackson Jr. and the late Betty G. Jackson were as patient with me as God is. They raised two children who turned out saved and are preachers. They did something *right*! I love them! So when I make the trip from West Virginia to DC to take my ninety-year-old dad shopping, it's my *duty*, my *honor*, and my *right* to do it for the man who sacrificed so much for me. It is my joy to do it. Even now, he still is parenting my sister and me. If he does not hear from us by a certain time, he worries. He will then say, "I didn't know whether you were laying down there with a tag on your toe or not." Then you know. Uh oh, you didn't make a call on time. You got Daddy worried. That's not good.

However, that is what being a part of the family village is about. He is the undisputed patriarch of the Jackson clan. He sits at the gate of the family village. He presides at the family meals. He pronounces the family blessings. He still speaks with prophetic wisdom over us, and we listen.

I see him smile through the constant pain of arthritis, which he lives with each and every day. If I could take that pain away from him, I would do it in a heartbeat. I wish there was more I could do for the man who has done so much for me. If I had millions of dollars, I would pour it at his feet. I know that is not what he would care about. What gives him joy is his family. He says he also tries to find something to laugh about every day. That keeps him going.

He is not only an elder in the family. He is a respected elder in his neighborhood. He lives just around the corner from the house in which he was raised, his grandmother's house (Nana's house). No one has ever lived there but a Jackson.

Sometimes I can almost see Nana, who passed in 1966; Grandma Jackson, who passed in 1973 (as did Grandma Graham); Granddaddy Jackson, who passed in 1980; Momma, who passed June 15, 2005; and Auntie, who passed June 20, 2005; all looking down and smiling at him as they are being held safe in the arms of Jesus. "Keep up the good work," they are saying. "Keep looking after our family. We see you through Jesus's eyes."

I don't know if I am considered the heir apparent or not. I do know the shoes of my dad will be some tough shoes to fill. I pray that day is yet a long way off. I pray that God keeps his pain from getting worse. I would love for Daddy to make it to one hundred. Aunt Belle lived to be one hundred and a half years old. I would love to hold a birthday celebration for Daddy on May 27, 2024! Only God knows. Keep smiling, Daddy! You keep me motivated.

The Family Tribal Heritage

We are the sum total of all of our parts, no matter how good or bad the experiences may be. Every family has its share of both. What makes for a good family is how you decide to work through your crises, your disagreements, and your issues. Good strong families work things out together. You may not always agree, but you must know how to love one another! That is what makes you a family.

I have shared a great deal about the family that I love. I have shared some humor, some of the sad moments, and many of our strengths. What I did not share and would never share are the short-comings or faults of any of us. Those things belong only to Christ and to that family member. One thing that I find appalling is families that air their dirty laundry in public for the world to see. I cringe when people go on television shows to discuss disgusting things that have gone on in their families before a national audience. For the sake of fame and a few dollars, they degrade the name of their family.

I don't understand many things. I don't understand how parents can mistreat their children, abandon them, or abuse them in whatever form that takes. Those things make no sense to me.

The only way we can pick our families is if we marry into them or we are adopted into them as when we come into the body of Christ. The word of God says, "You have not chosen Me, but I have chosen you and ordained you that you should go and bring forth fruit and that your fruit should remain: that whatsoever you shall ask of the Father in My name He may give you." (John 15:16) I know that God loves us so much that He does not put us down but affirms us. We should always affirm each other as members of our family. If we did that today, street gangs would not have the stronghold they do, nor would teen pregnancy, drugs, and some of the other things going on today.

When I hear of family members who have not spoken to each other in years because of something that was said or done out of turn, it grieves my spirit because that is not what Christ wants for us.

Along with trains, I have always had a fascination with wringer washing machines. I learned to wash clothes using one. When washing clothes in water too hot to touch with a bare hand, you would use a washing stick to pull the clothes out of the water. Some situations in our families are like that; they are too hot to handle. When I would hang clothes on the line outside, there were certain items I did not want the neighbors looking at because they were private.

Nobody back then had a dryer. Some of the neighbors didn't care what they hung on the line, but I was always protective of my family's personal garments. Either I hung them in the basement to dry or I would hang them outside between lines of sheets or other large items to block them from view. Everyone should adopt that protective mind-set about his or her family—affirming one another at all times to the world and privately working out any differences. These are things that make a family strong. They also make a church strong.

It is a sick church that has members who tear down brothers and sisters in Christ or the pastor and think they are doing God's will. If you are doing that, you are in sin. Does not Christ deal with you in love?

I am sure my parents were not always pleased with my behavior or my actions. I know there were times when I greatly disappointed them, as do all children. Many times, I was angry with myself because I disappointed them. There were things that I knew I did wrong but they never saw, and I punished myself because I knew they would not be pleased. How did I punish myself? It was by conviction because of what they had taught me. My conscience would eat at me if I did things I knew were wrong or of things of which my family would not approve. I never wanted to displease my parents or displease God. I would sometimes imagine stepping out of line and bringing tears to God's eyes. The thought of that made my heart very sad.

All of that upbringing went into my programming, into my DNA, into my thought processes, filtered by Christian teachings and sealed in place by the Holy Spirit.

Yes, like many youngsters, I rebelled against the teachings, fighting hard to be different. My rebellion was subtle. I was too scared to do things that could send me to jail. I was too afraid that my parents and aunts and uncles would send me to the morgue before the jailer came for me. Besides, there were enough spiritual chains trying to pull me down. Many of those chains were the work of people who were either jealous of what God had blessed me with or just plain wanted to pull me down. My rebellion was more in the style of worship

I sought. (That's another chapter.) The Holy Spirit, I guess, kept me from going too far. (I was also afraid to go too far.) Proverbs 22:6 says it best. "Train up a child in the way he should go: and when he is old, he will not depart from it."

I ended up not very far from the precepts and doctrines that were placed in me from my childhood. Some of where I was headed was too dogmatic, too legalistic, and too closed to what God was showing me. That was taking me away from the doctrine I was taught and what the Holy Spirit was showing my about how to be free in Christ. God wanted me to be free in Him to experience His love and liberty as well as to share it with others. I am sixty-four at the time of this writing, and I am not going anywhere. I am locked into my family and my Christ, my savior. *Case closed*!

2

EDUCATION AND THE EDUCATION THAT GOES WITH IT

Going to school at five years of age is traumatic! I had spent four good years bonding with a loving family; being babysat by Grandma and Granddaddy; and being taken on train trips to Baltimore during the day and to playgrounds with my cousin, DeLyse, by Uncle Sidney on his off days from being a chef on the B&O Railroad's Capitol Limited. (By the way, I thought it was *his* railroad.) Now, all of a sudden, I found out why I had been learning how to print my name and to know my address, my phone number, and Grandma and Granddaddy's phone number, as well as Nana's, who lived near Charles Young Elementary School.

By this time, I had developed an interest in trains, which would be a lifelong hobby. My favorite book was (and still is) *The Little Engine That Could* by Watty Piper. I had asked my mother to read it to me so often that she told me I would have to learn to read it for myself. So, looking at the pictures, I would tell myself the story over and over again. I will never forget that she told me that the book had a lesson. She said it was more than just a story about a little blue engine. She said that the story tells how you can do anything that you put your heart and mind to do, if you really believe in yourself. She told me that when I was four years old. At sixty-four, those words still ring in my ears. That was the lesson she taught me before I went to school.

I have a copy of the book, and I will never part with it. Often I have found myself like the little blue engine, having to tell myself, "I think I can. I think I can. I think I can." Sometimes, it's, "Jesus, help me, Jesus, help me, Jesus, help me." At a difficult time in my life, I was on a retreat weekend, and my mother wrote a note to me, reminding me of that story. I still have the note, though she has been with the Lord for nine years as of this writing. That note left me in a big ball of mush and tears. However, it reminded me that I was going to make it somehow with God's help.

That first day of school, Momma took me to Charles Young Elementary. My dad had gone to the school when it first opened in 1932. Here I was, going to kindergarten in 1955. We stopped at the office. I knew the principal from Nineteenth Street Baptist Church, Martha H. Winston. She was on the trustee board of the church with my grandfather. She was rather matronly and wore her salt-and-pepper hair pulled into a bun at the back of her head. She wore glasses. She wore bracelets that jingled. A little boy who looked absolutely horrified was sitting in her office. Mrs. Winston spoke to my mother briefly and said, "Excuse me; I have to deal with this little boy."

She grabbed a yardstick off her desk, took the little boy by the arm, pulled him out of his chair and into her private bathroom, and closed the door. The next sounds I heard were the yardstick making contact with the little boy's rear end and the boy crying. I could hear Miss Winston saying, "You will behave in my school for my teachers. Do you understand?"

"Yes, Miss. Winston," he responded.

My mother leaned down to me and whispered, "She better not ever have to bring you in here and spank you! If she does, you'll get another one when you get home! Do you understand me?" She did not have to worry about that. A double-header spanking was not something I would ever put on my agenda.

Miss Winston came out of the restroom and told the secretary, "Miss Jones, call Raymond's mother and ask her to bring him some clean pants. He just wet his clothes. Tell Mr. Greene he needs to come mop my floor again." Mrs. Winston made small talk with my mother about church for few minutes and then told her that I would be in Miss Carter's class. That was room 109. She was a good teacher and one of three kindergarten teachers. I would be in her morning class.

After telling me that she was glad to have me at her school, the principal asked if I had any questions. I only had one, after seeing and hearing all I had experienced of Raymond's episode. "Where can I go to the bathroom? I have to go really bad now."

After I had been thoroughly traumatized in the office, we walked past two other kindergarten rooms—Mrs. Wilson's room and the tall Miss Carter's room. Then we reached my classroom, the short Miss Carter's room. We were baby boomers. The classes were large— about thirty-six students in each kindergarten class. With six half-day classes, three in the morning and three in the afternoon, there were about 216 kindergarten students in the school in 1955. However, the teachers had control of the classes.

Kindergarten was fairly easy; we spent time learning how to play with others, to share, to finger paint, to color, to listen to stories, to sing "Jesus Loves Me," to say the Lord's Prayer, and to say grace. (We learned it *in the public school!*) I had already learned these things at home, as well as how to write my name and read some. The school discouraged my mother from working with me at home. Some of the kids mistook my hunger to learn as snobbery. Children can be so hurtful. I started to shut down.

We took field trips to places that were new to some of the children but not to me. I had been taken to the White House, the Washington Monument, the US Capitol, Union Station, the Jefferson Memorial, and the Lincoln Memorial. My parents, grandparents, aunt, and uncle had exposed me to these things on their days off. They had talked to my cousins and me about the history of these important buildings and monuments. When the kindergarten walked through the circus grounds, my parents and my aunt and uncle had already taken my cousins and me to the circus. (Cynthia was just an infant when I was in kindergarten.)

It is amazing that I can remember the names of all of my elementary school teachers when I sometimes can't remember what I ate for dinner. I started kindergarten with Miss Carter (the short one). Then she left, and Miss Dorey finished the year. First grade was Mrs. Chambers, whose husband was a motorcycle police officer. Mrs. Alexander was second grade. Then we moved to Upper Northeast DC and at Keene Elementary, I had Mrs. Jarrett for third grade and Mrs. Frank for fourth grade (she wore red shoes or blue shoes every day). I had Mrs. Tilton and then Miss E. L. Foster for fifth grade and Mrs. Jobe for sixth grade, with Miss Mildred P. Totten as a substitute while Mrs. Jobe was out sick.

I knew early in life that Jacksons and Grahams went to school to learn and not to be class clowns or behavior problems. None of us on either side of the family was a behavior problem. If a teacher called our parents for a conference, it was very rarely disciplinary reasons. It was just plain not acceptable on either side of the family. If you didn't understand something, it had better not be because you were not paying attention in class. You were expected to learn. The hope was that one day, segregation would end, and we would get really good jobs because we were smart enough to get them. We knew the unwritten law. You will have to work five times as hard to be recognized a third as often as others are. I would see this scenario played out many times in my life when I would become the "first African American" in several positions of employment. You are put under a high-powered microscope. You are scrutinized, dissected, and analyzed because no one like you has ever had that job before. You will be the measuring stick for any future people who look like you. Yet you will be told—with great sincerity—that it is not prejudice. One thing I learned: if something looks, waddles, quacks, and swims like a duck, nine times out of ten, it is a duck. I have learned to live and work with many duck mentalities.

I was talking with my father a couple of days before this writing, and we were discussing the monster of racial hatred and some of the ways it had shown itself in the military prior to integration and even in our nation's capital.

As a child, I used to wonder why, when we dressed up to go downtown, we only went to Kann's department store for clothes and Hahn's Shoes for shoes. They were the only stores that allowed African Americans to try on clothes and shoes, so they were the ones that got our business.

In the five-and-dime store in our neighborhood on H Street NE prior to integration, there was a section at the end of the food counter with no stools, where African Americans could stand and eat. At the other end of the counter, there were about fifteen seats. I would sometimes ask my mother if I could have a hot dog, and she would always answer sternly and in a dignified way, "You are not hungry enough to eat here!" I did not understand until years later what she was saying and what she was teaching me.

Not long after integration, seats were added at the end of the counter. She sat me down there one day and ordered a hot chocolate for me. She told me to sit there and drink it while she went downstairs to get some stockings. I was sipping my hot chocolate and stirring it with a spoon when the server walked over, put her hand over my cup, got down in my face, and said, "I hate that I have to serve you, you little pickaninny". (I didn't know what that was, but by the way she said it, I did know it probably was not a nice name.) When she tried to take my hot chocolate, I bit her with my little, razor-sharp, four-year-old teeth. I don't know what made me bite her; I was not a biter. As I held on for dear life to the hot chocolate that my mother had bought for me, there was such a commotion that my mother must have heard the noise.

The manager got the server away from the counter, wiped up the splatters of hot chocolate, and quickly poured a little more in my cup. My mother came running back to the counter with her stockings and asked, "Did something happen?"

The manager looked quickly at me and shook his head. Then I said, "No, Mommy." The manager gave my mother a cup of coffee. Thirty-five years later, I told my mother why she got that free coffee at the Five and Dime Store. She remembered the day. She had heard some noise and thought she'd better get back to her child at the counter.

Beware of the Monsters! (An Education within the Education)
I guess my shutdown started in the middle of kindergarten. Monsters stole some of the joy of school from me. There were monsters at school who would say, "You think you are better than us because you have been to this place or that." I never thought that. I just wanted to share it with them.

There were monsters who would say, "You think you are better than us because you use words like grown people! Why don't you just shut up? You make me sick!" I simply had been taught to speak distinctly and enunciate my words.

The monsters eventually became internal. They began to silence me, cloud my thoughts, stifle creativity, steal my brightness, and quiet the song in my heart. So I would get quiet at school even though I knew the answer because I just didn't want another attack from the monsters. There are monsters that go to school that we call bullies. There are neighborhood bullies, there are work bullies, and there are church bullies. What they all have in common is that they are monsters. The monsters can be found everywhere. I struggled through school—particularly junior high school, which is now called middle school. However, I got an A in "monsterology."

It is true that the monsters cause you to be sick in spirit and in soul. However, the truth of the matter is that the monsters are themselves extremely sick. When one person denigrates another person to affirm himself, that is a sickness. The more he does it, the sicker he is.

I have never liked confusion, fights, or drama. Once some people know that about you, they deliberately try to spark those things just to unsettle your life. Monsters (that's what bullies are) thrive on all of the above. They thrive on creating and maintaining those things in the lives of their chosen victims.

I am a very easygoing, laid-back person. I work hard to keep myself under control because I know I am like my favorite type of railroad engine, a steam locomotive. Trains have been my hobby since I was three years old. A steam locomotive is big and powerful and beautiful. To me, it is the most beautiful type of railroad equipment ever built. However, since it runs on steam, it can be dangerous if you are not careful and do not watch the pressure gauges to maintain the proper water and steam pressure in relation to the fire and heat in the firebox. If the fire is too hot, the steam pressure too high, and the water level in the boiler is too low, you can have a boiler explosion.

That describes me and anyone else who is patient, internalizes things, does not talk much about issues, and takes a lot of abuse. Then one day, you just explode. You read about these people every day in newspapers and see them on the news. They are children who have been bullied in school and housewives who have been beaten one time too many. Yes, that happens to husbands too. Don't think it doesn't. They are children who have been sexually assaulted one time too many and whose cries for help have been ignored by the legal or social service system. They are congregations in which the church bully has gone one step too far. These are things you see and read about. You hear the horror stories every day. But for every story that you hear, there are probably hundreds that you will never know.

As I mentioned, I try to avoid conflict at all cost. It is just not healthy. In fifth grade, a boy who lived nearby walked to and from school with me, and we walked home for lunch together. (We did that back then in DC.) We got along fine until I made friends with someone who moved in around the corner from him. I am not mentioning their names out of respect for them and the lives they now live, wherever they are. (I will not mention anyone's name in a negative light, even if he or she is a person I have no further dealings with or who has done me harm.) The first boy became angry because he didn't like my new friend. I don't know what happened, but my new friend's parents had talked with his parents, and he was forbidden to have anything to do with my new friend. He then directed his anger to me. It started with verbal assaults. Then it was pushing and shoving. When I pushed back, he got a little group to help him. Bullies never act alone. They always do their best taunting with an audience or a following. This boy was thin, and his skin was medium brown with a sort of reddish hue. I say that because of what I am about to tell you.

I had been altering my trips home from school to avoid these monsters, who would intercept me on my journey to punch me, kick me, call me names, or whatever else they chose to do for fun that day. My new friend had stopped walking home from school with me out of fear. On this particular day, I had a strange feeling that the skinny little monster and his buddies had some serious taunting planned. He had been whispering to some bigger boys—sixth graders—at recess, and his group of three boys had grown to about ten. They were waiting for me outside the door I usually used.

So, I went out the back door and across the playground in the opposite direction. I walked two streets over, through a small wooded area, to the B&O Railroad tracks. I knew I was not to cross, walk on, play on, or go anywhere near the railroad tracks. That was the school rule and the rule at home. However, at that point, I preferred facing a sound spanking and punishment at home to being ganged up on by a bunch of sixth graders with that fourth grader.

I ran for dear life. My heart was pounding. I left the tracks near my home and walked through another wooded area. I looked to see if the gang was there or if either of my parents was driving by. (You never know when a parent might leave work early.) I don't remember when I grabbed the long, thin, green stick I was carrying. However, I was so scared that I was determined that if they cornered me and hurt me, I was going to leave some evidence that I had tried to fend them off.

Two blocks from home, running as hard as I could, I was ambushed by that skinny monster and his gang of sixth-grade thugs.

"Where are you going, four eyes?" he said as he punched me in my chest. His buddies laughed and said, "Hit him again."

His eyes were full of hatred. I had done nothing to him. I don't know why he hated my guts so much. I didn't know his sixth-grade thug friends at all. I do know that I had had *enough*! The only thing I remember was seeing him draw back his skinny fist. Before he could land his punch, I swung that stick I was carrying. I don't know how many times I swung it. I don't know how many kids I hit. My focus was on the one in front of me—the skinny, slightly taller, fourth-grade boy who had taunted me for months. My heart was beating fast. The big boys tried to hit me, but the stick was moving too fast. I was swinging it like a whip. You could hear it whistle and snap as it landed. The skinny boy in front of me was catching the worst of it. I was screaming bloody murder and crying with fear and trembling. I remember screaming, "Why don't you leave me alone!"

I must have hit him in his face once. A wide auburn-red welt ran across his left cheek, from his ear to the middle of his neck. His fist opened, and he grabbed his face. He was now screaming too. The sixth graders took off running. I took off after them, screaming and crying and still swinging the stick. I must have landed a couple more hits before I made my last turn and ran home.

I was in hysterics when I got home. I was crying so hard I could not even tell Grandma Graham what had happened. Thank God for nosy neighbors. As fate would have it, one of the neighbors had observed the taunting from her living room window for several days. She had seen me being chased home, hit, kicked, tripped, and even spit at. She called the boy's parents and told them what he had been doing and what had happened that day after school. His parents came to my house to have a talk with mine. I just knew I was going to get it. I waited in my bedroom for the worst.

But the worst never came. What did come was a talk about how you should tell your parents if you are having troubles. I went to bed early that night, not because I was in trouble but because I was so drained. Ironically, I had become very sick too. That illness probably had been coming on for a couple of days. I guess there is some truth to the theory that a sick or wounded animal is the most dangerous. I was dangerous that day. That monster was defeated. When I got back to school, I never had a problem with the sixth graders again. That fourth grader had other problems, also. I think he ended up in the National Training School for Boys, which used to stand high on a hill at Bladensburg Road and South Dakota Avenue NE. I'd always been told that was where they send little boys who don't know how to behave at home. It is gone now. Condominiums, townhouses, and a funeral home now occupy the ground where it stood. There is a cemetery there, too. I believe it was always there, in front of the training school. My mother is buried in that cemetery.

There were more monsters in junior high and some in high school. I wanted to go to a high school across town by special permission, but my parents said no. They said I needed to learn to live with all kinds of people. I made a mental note for myself for when I was an adult. There were certain things I was not going to do, certain types of people I did not need as friends, and certain places I would never live.

I knew from watching the news in the 1960s that there were certain places in the South I did not want to live or visit. I saw some of the monster behavior acted out during the civil rights movement.

The other side of that coin is when people don't respect themselves and use with each other in conversation and in music the same racial slurs and epithets that our ancestors fought so hard to liberate us from. Using those words helps to keep monsters alive. No one is to blame for that but us, then. If you want a behavior to change, you can't just say it; you have to model the change.

I saw a couple of college bullies, too. One was even professor. He walked into the classroom, looked around, and said, "Most of you have nothing to worry about because if I like you, you will pass my class. However, the most some of you will get out of me will be a D, no matter what you do. If I like you, you'll pass; and if I don't like you, you'll fail." Then he leaned down into my face and said, "Do you catch my drift?"

Not only did I catch it, but Ray Charles and Stevie Wonder could have seen it! That left me bitter on my first day of college. It caused me to change my major. It altered the course of my life and created some mental blocks that even today I am still working through. That is the stuff that monsters do.

Those school monsters left deep impressions on me. When I started working in the school system, I had zero tolerance for bullies.

Your Education Is the Hope of Your Ancestors
First, I want to say that I do not believe in looking down on people who have not gone to college. One can have a good education and be very knowledgeable in an area of expertise that is beneficial to the economy and to society without going to college. It bothers me when I see college professors or classroom teachers look down their noses at the people who keep their classrooms clean and make the environment conducive for learning. What if the cafeteria worker was not skilled in ServSafe and food-handling practices? What if the orderly in the hospital was not skilled in cleaning an operating room? Do you not realize how many infectious diseases they prevent by knowing how to do their jobs well?

I thought my grandma Graham ran the nursing home in which she was a caregiver, and my parents, aunts, and uncles ran the federal government as Miss Martha H. Winston ran Charles Young Elementary School because of their work ethic. They took ownership of what they did and pride in their work. That is missing at every level of our society today, it is sad to say. Where are the skilled craftsmen, the skilled laborers, and others who took pride in providing quality work and service with dignity and integrity?

Members of my family worked hard, struggled, and made sacrifices for their children because they wanted us to go beyond where they were allowed to go. They wanted us to be equipped for jobs they were denied because of the color of their skin.

My great-grandfather William Myree was one of my grandma Graham's teachers in a one-room schoolhouse in Alabama. Grandma left school at the end of eighth grade because her mother was in poor health, and as the oldest child, she had to assist in taking care of her brothers and sisters. One of my great-aunts (Aunt Annie) grew up to be the principal of a school. Grandma had made sacrifices early. Others in the family had done similar things so that others could forge ahead. Grandma never lived to see her three youngest children attend college as senior citizens. Momma had enough courses for a degree but all in different areas. Aunt Cinnie obtained a bachelor's degree in Christian education when she was in her late fifties. Uncle Glenn obtained a master's degree as a senior, well after high school. I look at my sister, who can find you detailed information on any subject you want on the web. Man, can she dig out information! Those years she spent in law enforcement in the DC police department really paid off! Now that she is in the ministry and we share things, she'll start rattling off what she found about the Hebrew or the Greek root of something, and it makes me ask her where she found it. (I led her to Christ!) My cousins have all managed to make a mark in whatever field they chose to pursue.

Yes, our elders wanted us to go where they weren't allowed to go.

Models and Motivations

After poet Maya Angelou's death, I wrote a tribute to her for my friend Pastor David Housholder's Life and Liberty website. In response, my friend Jen Clark Tinker shared a video of Oprah Winfrey's interview with Maya Angelou. In it, Ms. Angelou talked about how her mother motivated her and pushed her to pursue a job as a streetcar conductor, which was unheard of for a black woman at that time. She was the first.

Listening to this conversation between these two women whom I greatly admire for the things they have done and their literary and creative genius, I was moved to write again after years of letting the monsters in my life shut me down. Whether anything comes of this book or not, as I write, I am killing another school monster who said, "He thinks he's so smart." I can't help it that my imagination gave me ideas. Was it my fault that a teacher wanted to hear what I was writing?

My assistant pastor, Rev. Dr. Donald F. Taylor, has begun writing. He started long before I did. In one of our conversations, he said, "Rev. Walter Jackson, *my* pastor, you have had a wealth of experiences. Don't let all of that go to the grave with you. Document these things from your parents and your grandparents. You have *no* idea how valuable that is." He and David are world travelers. When they began to push—along with Jen and my sister—I figured that I'd better listen, even if this book never gets any farther than my thumb drive. At least I will have put it down as my mother did with her poems, as I once did with songs, and as I do every week with sermon outlines for my small-town congregation. I must also add to this list of encouragers Dr. James Harrison, executive minister of the American Baptist Churches of the South (ABCOTS). It is one of thirty-five regions of American Baptist Churches USA. On several occasions, his encouragement has kept me going. He is a true pastor motivator.

Though I have not yet told my dad that I am writing a book, I have asked him some questions about family history as I have Uncle Glenn. Daddy has a certain spirit about him that lets you feel when he is proud of you. I feel that every time I take him to the store or share a sermon topic with him. I think he knows I am up to something. I felt that spirit the other day when I asked him a question about his elementary school. He's my dad. He knows I am up to something. He may tell my sister, "Your brother was asking me questions about when I went to school. That boy is up to something. I know you know what it is." She'll eventually call me and say, "You've been *busted!*"

I love the way he motivates me and pushes me without my knowledge that I am being pushed until I'm out there! Then he smiles and shakes his head. Yeah, I know him, too!

I can hear my mother saying, "A job worth doing is worth doing well." Even now, I can feel my grandma Graham sitting behind me as she would do when I had homework to finish after dinner and it was late. There were times in junior high and high school that I had so much homework that it would be past my normal bedtime—and past hers, too. She would sit in the chair with her Bible, reading. If I nodded off, she would encourage me, saying, "Keep at it." She wouldn't go to bed until I had closed my textbooks and was ready to go upstairs.

In elementary school, Grandma Jackson would give me homemade gingerbread, or pound cake and Jell-O, and Granddaddy would come and ask if I understood my lessons. They pushed, encouraged, and strengthened. They did the same for my parents, giving them breaks when they felt they were overwhelmed. I can feel them now, sitting right behind me. I can almost smell the gingerbread, hear Grandma Graham saying, "Keep at it!" and Granddaddy Jackson asking, "Did you understand your lessons?" Others who are with Jesus are with them behind me. These are people I will never forget; they are the people who kept me going, even when I didn't feel like it: Martha H. Winston; Gussie E. Baylor and Barbara King (two of my late deaconesses); Dorothy Louise Amanda Randolph Johnson (the late mother of the church); Louise Rogers (a late trustee of the church); my godparents, James and Lillie Mae Glenn; Uncle Louis; Aunt Cinnie; Aunt Katie; Uncle Morris; Uncle Zetty; Auntie; and all of those in my family who paved the way for me to make it this far by faith. Because of them, I am still learning even now how to eliminate monsters as they arise. I am still working on preventing some of those monsters from having influence in my life. Their influence is a stronghold. Strongholds are bondage. Bondage is not of God, it is of Satan and his demonic forces. I have learned other ways to deal with them now. I have learned that some monsters, God does not move; He just declaws them, defangs them, or makes others immune to their venom until He is ready to neutralize them.

I had role models in school, such as my seventh-grade science teacher, Miss DeVaule. She made science so much fun that I stayed after school to help her set up the class for the next day. I had never dissected an animal, other than gutting fish, until I got to her class. I was fascinated by dissecting a shark loaded with baby sharks, a bullfrog, a fetal pig, and a cat that had four kittens inside. I would stay after school on purpose to help her and to avoid the monsters from my last-period gym class who were angry because they lost an intramural basketball game or football game because I was on their team. To this day, I am not a fan of baseball, basketball, or football because of those monsters. My sports are swimming, bicycling, weightlifting, and bowling, none of which we did then.

Miss DeVaule would take me with her to return movies downtown and then drop me off at home. She would take me to Cedar Knoll Cemetery, which was across the road from where my grandma Jackson, Cousin Vernon, Granddaddy Jackson, Auntie, Nana, and Aunt Belle would later be buried, to catch tadpoles that the class could observe turning into frogs. She gave me a love for science. At the end of the school year, she gave me all of the guppies in her fish tank. Thirty years later, I still had offspring from those original guppies. I still have the fish tanks. When I started as a school librarian in Jefferson County, I set up my fish tank and incorporated it into teaching library skills. I used it to teach pre kindergarteners how to feed the fish as part of our library exercise before our stories. We would talk about the colors of the fish. They got excited when the guppies had babies. (They are live bearers!) I used them to teach about ecosystems at South Jefferson Elementary when I started there four years ago. I told the students about my favorite science teacher, Miss DeVaule from Kramer Junior High in Washington, DC. I don't know whether she is living or dead, but she will remain very much alive in my spirit and love of science.

If I was not hanging out with Miss DeVaule, by ninth grade I was hanging out in Mr. Atruss Fleming's room. He taught music and ninth-grade chorus. I was fascinated by music because it played a big part in my family. By this time, many of my junior high monsters had been sent to the National Training School for Boys. One had been killed by the police during a robbery not far from the school. I figured out to ignore the rest of them.

I didn't know it at the time, but Mr. Fleming was an accomplished pianist, organist, composer, and arranger in the DC area. In ninth-grade chorus, we sang the same kinds of songs I'd learned at church as well as some others, such as "Ava Verum Corpus" (yes, he taught it to us in Latin) and "This is My Country" (we sang *his* arrangement). I shall never forget the day one of the boys in the choir said, "Mr. Fleming, why are we singing this? It is *not* our country. We can't sit in restaurants in the South and in some places in the North without problems. Our parents can't get the same jobs as other people. They are beating black people up and killing them for trying to register to vote. They killed Medgar Evers and those little girls in church in Alabama. Look at what happened in Selma, Alabama. Why are *we* singing *this* song? It is *not* our country!"

Mr. Fleming stood up from the piano and said, "Son, I cannot argue the facts of what you say that are happening. We have all seen it on TV, and some of you have lived it! However, we *will* sing it, and you *will* sing it with feeling, in hopes that one day, there *will* be a time when you *can* say this is *my country, land of my birth* and you will be able to sing it with pride and dignity and not *shame!*" He sat down again at the piano.

There was a moment of silence that seemed like an eternity. I could see the monsters of burning crosses, of fire hoses turned on full blast and blowing people off their feet and half a block down the street, of Bull Connor's venomous ax-handle rages, and of white-sheet brigades with Confederate flags, which, to African Americans, are the same as swastikas are to Jewish people. Yet we sang "This Is My Country" as Mr. Fleming wanted. We sang it as if that day had already arrived. Some of us, though we were only thirteen or fourteen years old, sang it with tears in our eyes. But sing we did. I believe he had water in his eyes, too, as he played the piano. *One day*, I pray that day will come when, as Mr. Fleming said, that monster will be gone forever.

We sang that song during our ninth-grade end-of-year concert and received a standing ovation. I am not sure if it was for his arrangement of the song, our performance, or both. I will never forget the lesson he taught us in his first-floor classroom that day in rehearsal as long as I live.

Sometime during the middle of eighth grade, for the second time in my school career, I knew I had no chance of ever getting into trouble at school, even if I wanted to. This was the year that Motown's Martha and the Vandellas released the hit "Nowhere to Run, Nowhere to Hide." Now, another member of Nineteenth Street Baptist Church was an administrator at my school. The pastor's wife,

Ettyce H. Moore, was now the assistant principal. Ironically, Miss Winston retired from Charles Young Elementary School the same year. Just as Miss Winston was on the trustee board with my grandfather, Mrs. Moore had grown up in the church with my father and sang in the choir with both of my parents. I had nowhere to run and nowhere to hide. However, I was not a behavior problem. Mrs. Moore was always on cafeteria duty during my lunch period. I think she liked coming by to tease me. She would stop to see if I had finished my lunch. If there was anything left on my tray, she would say, "Don't let me tell Lil Jack and Betty you didn't finish your vegetables." (My dad's nickname at church was Little Jack, and Granddaddy was Poppa Jack. I was called Little Walter for the longest time.) I would quickly tell her that I would eat them. It took me some time to realize that she was actually keeping tabs on other kids at that table, not me. One girl, who was constantly in her office for one thing or another, told me, "She is on a first-name basis with your mom and dad! I sure hope she doesn't get to know mine that well!"

Then it dawned on me that Mrs. Moore was indirectly letting this girl and some of her friends know that she was watching them by finding a reason to say something to me or to one of my friends, whose mother was a teaching colleague. We were a part of her disciplinary strategy. And no one messed with us at lunch, either.

Since I have mentioned Mrs. Ettyce H. Moore, who just recently passed away, as one of those education models and motivators, I must also mention her husband, the retired pastor of the Nineteenth Street Baptist Church, Rev. Dr. Jerry A. Moore Jr. He performed my parents' wedding service and blessed my sister, my cousins, and me as infants. He officiated at the funerals of my cousin Vernon, my grandparents, Uncle Sidney, my mother, and Auntie (five days later). At the time of this writing, he is almost one hundred years old. He taught me lessons about the church, the pastorate, pulpit decorum, Baptist Church polity, policy, and procedure that have remained with me to this day.

I have gone places and seen things that make me shake my head. When I have attempted to show people that things they are doing are wrong, according to church doctrine, or when deacons attempt to take away a member's rights and privileges or a pastor's responsibilities, and I get responses like, "We've never done it that way" or "That works in the city, but it won't work here," it makes me want to scream. Yes, each Baptist church is its own sovereign body. However, certain doctrines and covenants are standard. Reverend Moore made sure I learned all these things. I saw him take time with the children, greeting them on Sunday morning after church and at church picnics and other functions. My sister, Cynthia, said that at one time, she thought he was Jesus. Maybe that is why her baptism was such an interesting event.

Walking on Water

I have mentioned some things about my "beloved sister," Cynthia. (That term is an inside joke between us that struck a nerve with her, and we sometimes kid each other with it as we heal from past situations.) The story of her baptism stands out as a monumental moment for me.

Here we were on the first Sunday of the month, which was also Communion Sunday. Grandma Jackson had been assigned to assist her granddaughter. Cynthia had come out of the ladies' choir room dressed in the white baptismal robe and a white bathing cap to keep her hair dry. The year was somewhere around 1963 because we had moved from Northeast DC to Southeast DC. and Cynthia had just turned nine years old.

Cynthia sat in the front row with the deacons; Grandma Jackson was sitting behind her. Momma was a deaconess then, and Daddy was a deacon. Grandma Graham had moved to DC, and though she had joined Canaan Baptist with Aunt Belle, they were both sitting in the second row, as visiting deaconesses, alongside Grandma Jackson. I perched in the corner seat of the front row of the Jackson pew in the balcony, where I had a bird's-eye view when folks would be laid back in the water, symbolizing being buried with Christ and resurrected with Christ. I didn't fully understand the meaning of this event then, even though I had willingly made that step on July 7, 1957, at the age of seven. I understand it very well now!

The baptismal pool (some people call it a baptistery) was under the floor of the pulpit. The carpet and padding had been rolled up and pulpit chairs had been moved to the main floor. The podium was set off to the side for the pastor's use in opening worship and reading the baptismal responsive reading before he stepped down into the water for baptism. After Reverend Moore had led the congregation in the responsive reading and prayed in his very eloquent, melodious, well-trained Morehouse College way, he proceeded to step down into the baptismal pool as the choir began to sing,

> Take me to the water,
> Take me to the water,
> Take me to the water
> To be baptized.
> None but the righteous,
> None but the righteous,
> None but the righteous
> Shall see God.

Normally, the candidate for baptism is slowly escorted from his or her seat by a deacon or deaconess up to the pulpit and down the steps to the pastor waiting in the pool.

But this baptism was different from any other I had seen. At this baptism, I saw a miracle! At this baptism, I got a picture and a recount of the miracle of Jesus walking on water. Cynthia took one step down from the pulpit and then leaped into Rev. Dr. Jerry A. Moore's arms, locking her arms around his neck and her legs around his waist. She had climbed him like a tree. Had he been a short man, they both would have been under water. Not even the hem of her white baptismal robe touched the water in the pool!

It was a miracle, I thought. Cynthia had walked on water as Peter did! Had Reverend Moore said, "Come," like Jesus said to Peter? If he hadn't, Cynthia went anyway! The choir kept singing. Usually, two verses got you baptized. For Cynthia, it took four!

> I know I've got religion,
> I know I've got religion,
> I know I've got religion
> To be baptized.
> I know I've been converted,
> I know I've been converted,
> I know I've been converted
> To be baptized.

Reverend Moore was as cool as an early cucumber. He calmly raised his right hand as if nothing unusual had happened and said, "In obedience to the great command and upon the profession of your faith, I baptize you my sister in the name of the Father, the Son, and the Holy Ghost."

He then reached up very calmly, pried Cynthia's hands and feet loose, dropped her in the water, picked her right up, and handed her off to Grandma and Momma, who had by now stepped into the choir room and were watching from a doorway that was normally concealed behind the pulpit paneling. He handed her off so fast that her feet barely realized she was airborne. That was the coolest baptism I had ever seen.

Then Aunt Belle let out a holler and fainted clean out. I looked down and saw Grandma Graham trying to fan her with one of those funeral-home fans. The deaconess on whom Aunt Belle had swooned was trying to sit her upright. That was a sight. That sort of thing just didn't happen at the Nineteenth Street Baptist Church, just three blocks from the White House! For a moment, I thought I was at Mount Zion in Youngstown or at Mount Olive in Rectortown. Now, baptism was over and the choir was singing,

Hallelujah 'tis done,
I believe in the Son,
I've been saved by the blood of the crucified one.
Hallelujah 'tis done,
I believe in the Son,
I've been saved by the blood of the crucified one.

Later, the whole family got together at Grandma and Granddaddy Jackson's for dinner to celebrate the "new birth" experience. Grandma Graham asked Cynthia, "Baby, what happened to you? Did the Spirit take hold to you?"

Cynthia said, "No, Grandma, I was *scared*!"

Remember I told you that one thing we were taught to do was to tell the truth?

I was so impressed that Rev. Dr. Jerry Moore never lost his composure. It was so funny how he just pried Cynthia loose, dropped her, and then quickly grabbed her back and handed her off. I learned how to handle the baptisms of people who are deathly afraid of water from watching him baptize my sister. Though I have never had to drop anyone in the water, I have had to whisper, "Trust me, I won't let the water cover your face. I promise. This is a symbol, not a drowning." I quickly take them back and then up while they are smiling, and then I whisper, "See? I told you!"

I learned from Rev. Dr. Jerry Moore that there are those who will do everything they can to fight your vision for the growth of the church. He taught me that some will be against everything you do, but you have to trust God. After he had been at Nineteenth Street Baptist for forty-plus years, he told me, "I am just now beginning to see much of what I hoped to put into place." He taught me that it takes time to grow the people of God. You can only cause to grow the people who want to grow. You can only lead the people who want you to and will allow you to lead them. For years, I watched him struggle to move the historic church to a place where it could continue to grow in spite of those who wanted it to stay in a location where it could not expand and meet the needs of a growing ministry and congregation.

I learned from him how to give comfort to a grieving family during a time of loss and how to deliver a eulogy that helps a family get some closure, begin to pick up the pieces of their shattered lives, and move on, even when the loss of a loved one is extremely painful. Even though sometimes it is hard to detach yourself from the people and the situation you are ministering to because you have developed a bond with them, you have to find a way to give them comfort and strength. That is what God has called you to do as a pastor.

Rev. Dr. Jerry A. Moore taught me the upscale side of ministry, including proper protocol and even how to sit in the pulpit and not look like a slothful bum. I learned that the pulpit is a place where God reveals His word to His servant/vessel to deliver to the people of God. There is a certain way you carry yourself in that holy place. I know that today, many churches are more relaxed and laid-back in their approach to pulpit decorum. That is just not me.

Five other pastors played a tremendous part in my spiritual growth. Their preaching styles all were slightly different, but they were giants in ministry. They are the late Rev. W. A. Clark, who was the pastor at Mount Zion Baptist Church in Youngstown, Ohio; Rev. Dr. Norman Smith, who is pastor emeritus of the Mount Olive Baptist Church in Rectortown, Virginia; the late Rev. Dr. Benjamin Simmons, who was pastor of Christ Memorial Baptist Church in Philadelphia; Rev. Lonnie A. Simon, pastor emeritus of New Bethel Baptist Church in Youngstown; and one of my close friends, the late Rev. Nathaniel Woods, who served as my vice moderator of the Winchester Semiannual Meeting of the Brackett-Morrell Association (Area 7 of the American Baptist Churches of the South).

I spent summers in Youngstown listening to Reverend Clark's sermons. He had a somewhat gravelly voice and a style of preaching that was like singing, with a lot of moving. He had been my mother's pastor when she was a child. He baptized her, my aunt, and all of my uncles, to my knowledge. He was a kind man who loved his congregation. When I was licensed to preach and went to visit Youngstown, he would always say, "Why don't you preach for me tomorrow?" or "Preach for me this morning." I was only twenty years old. But he gave me an opportunity to preach in the pulpit where God had placed him. He didn't have to do that. I respected those invitations. Never once did I do anything to disgrace him. I did not talk about him, listen to, or participate in gossip about him. My World War II dad calls gossip "latrine talk"; it's conversation that has a stench to it.

Reverend Clark used to say, "Be treating everybody right because you don't know whose hand you're going to fall into." I never forgot that advice. It is so very true. I loved the energy he put into his preaching—his feeling and his conviction.

Rev. Dr. Norman Smith at Mount Olive Baptist was included in the Grant family gatherings. I got to see him not only at the church but also in our family setting. I learned from him how a pastor is to act when visiting church members. His style of preaching is very polished. Even though health issues have slowed him down, he is respected as a denominational leader among Baptists in Northern Virginia and among other church leaders as well. On the third Sunday in July this year, he was at the homecoming service, sitting next to Mrs. Smith. It was very hard to see him in a wheelchair. However, he still stands tall in my eyes. He led an old song that he loves, "Stay on the Rock." I had not heard it in years and had not heard *him* sing it in even more years. The words of the chorus go like this:

> Stay on the rock,
> Stay on the rock,
> Stay on the rock just a little while longer.
> Stay on the rock,
> Stay on the rock,
> Stay on the rock a little longer.

I looked down at him from where I sat at the pulpit and reflected back on all the times I'd heard him sing that song when I was a child. The congregation helped him with the chorus, tapping their feet on the wooden floor, as they did in years gone by. I closed my eyes, and I could see my great-uncle Rob, Aunt Edmonia, Cousin Foster, Cousin Virginia, my grandmother and grandfather, and the rest of the Grant side of the family who are now in the arms of Jesus, sitting in the pews like they once did, singing and encouraging us to "stay on the rock a little longer," the rock being Christ Jesus. Reverend Smith, though weak in body, still sang with power just as he used to preach.

When I went to college outside of Philadelphia for two years, I wanted to find a church like Mount Zion and Mount Olive. The churches near the college were a little too "dry" for what I wanted in worship. I guess that was my form of rebellion. I didn't want a quiet church in college. Other students rebelled in more conventional ways, by not going to church at all (and we were at a Christian college) or by becoming extremely wild. My rebellion was to go to what I considered a fiery church with very spirited worship. I found that at the Christ Memorial Baptist Church on the corner of Germantown Avenue and Susquehanna Avenue. Rev. Benjamin Simmons was the founder and the pastor.

The church was like a theater inside. However, I think it had been an old union hall with a stage and plenty of theater seats. The members had built out the stage, turning it into a choir stand, and built the pulpit a little lower. Off to the right, if you were facing the pulpit area, they had built a baptismal pool.

After I was licensed to preach, Reverend Simmons used me every Sunday to assist as worship leader. I got practice doing responsive readings and reading scripture. I also ended up working with the choir as one of the assistant pianist/assistant directors. I learned more common-meter songs. He liked to sing a song called "I Believe I'll Run On and See What the End's Going to Be." I had never heard that one before. Different congregations in the South sang some different common-meter songs or sang the songs a little differently.

Like my family in Youngstown, many of the members of that church had come from the South. Reverend Simmons had come north to Philadelphia from Florida. Others had come from Georgia, Alabama, Mississippi, North Carolina, South Carolina, and Arkansas. Worship at Christ Memorial had a different flare than it did in Youngstown. It was spirited, but it had more of an urban flavor.

Reverend Simmons had me preach on occasion, and like Reverend Clark and Reverend Smith, I could tell he had a genuine love for the members. These men were not "bully" pastors. Yes, some pastors can be monsters. I will not mention any of them at all. All of the pastors that I mention by name are—or were, if they are deceased—loving, compassionate people, whom, I believe, God will reward greatly.

Rev. Lonnie Simon was pastor (now retired) of the New Bethel Baptist Church in Youngstown, Ohio. When my uncle Louis and aunt Cinnie changed churches, they became members of the New Bethel Baptist Church and became just as active as they had been at Mount Zion Baptist Church. Reverend Simon had been a bowling buddy of my uncle's. They also had sung together in a gospel quartet. They were very big at one time. Reverend Simon's style of preaching is full of energy in much the same way as Reverend Clark's had been and in the style of Reverend Smith.

Two years in a row, my good friend, the late Rev. Nathaniel Woods, who had grown up with Reverend Simon, and I invited him to our churches (which were only twelve miles apart) to hold a joint revival. One thing about a revival is that the results always seem to occur after the revival is over. After one of those revivals, I baptized my daughter and her godfather, and people started bringing Bibles to church. Reverend Simon had preached, "The Bible is like your sword. Everybody should carry their weapon to fight off the devil. If you can't carry a full sword, carry your switchblade (a New Testament)." That statement stuck with people, and it stuck with me.

Reverend Woods and his wife, Clarice, had become very good friends of mine when he became the pastor of a church in our association. At that time, the Woodses and I lived in the DC suburbs and often traveled to meetings and conventions together. I also was the pianist for several recitals that Mrs. Woods performed. The unique thing about our friendship was that we were not close in age. Reverend Woods and my mother were the exact same age. However, he and I were the best of friends. When I became the moderator of the Winchester Semiannual Meeting of the Brackett-Morrell Association, he became the vice moderator. We were a great team. We planned and had visions of what our churches could do for the cause of Christ.

Four times, we traveled together by train and rental car to conventions of the American Baptist Churches of the South in Miami, New Orleans, Baton Rouge, and Atlanta. We traveled by car together to Brackett-Morrell Association meetings hosted by our sister churches in Roanoke and Luray, Virginia, and stayed over in hotels to keep from commuting when our churches hosted the meetings on those weekends. We had many good times, laughing in fellowship and praising God when the anointing would hit. When Rev. Dr. Eugene Johnson, who now is pastor of Mount Olive Baptist Church in Centerville, Virginia, became the pastor of one of the churches in our association, he became part of our "trio of pastor hang-out buddies." At meetings and conventions, when you saw one of us, you saw all three, Jackson, Woods, and Johnson. The late mother of our church, Deaconess Gussie E. Baylor, would say that we were always up to something. She affectionately called us "her three little bad boys." She liked the fact that the three of us had such a close bond of friendship and fellowship.

I remember one time at one of the churches in the association (Lovely Zion in Bedford, Virginia, I believe), Reverend Johnson was preaching and doing such a tremendous job that Reverend Woods was egging him on from one side of the pulpit, and I was on the other side, doing the same. Reverend Johnson could hardly get the words out of his mouth. Reverend Woods and I were so in tune with what he was saying that we were helping him finish his sentences. As Reverend Johnson was nearing the end of his sermon, his preaching got more intense. The spirit was high.

Reverend Woods leaped to his feet. He had this way of feeling the spirit that caused him to look like he was in the eye of a tornado. My daughter used to call it "the Reverend Woods twist." I never should have tried to steady Reverend Woods on his feet, but I reached out to hold his arm so he wouldn't dance in the spirit right off the pulpit. It was as though I had grabbed a live electrical wire while standing in water. Then, there we were, all three of us caught up in the spirit. Reverend Johnson was expending a big surge of energy, bringing his sermon to a close, while Reverend Woods and I were behind him on the pulpit having what would be called in some African American Baptist or Pentecostal churches a "sanctified Holy Ghost fit."

I remember Mrs. Woods and Mrs. Johnson saying that none of us was in any shape to help the others. We three had entered "the praise zone." It's a rare occasion when you become so caught up in worship that you just get lost in the presence of God. This must be like what Moses felt and experienced when God placed him in the crevice of the rock, covered his face with His hand, and walked past him, declaring His name and allowing Moses to see His back.

When Reverend Woods passed away suddenly while he was on vacation, I was so devastated that I cried for three days. I could not even bring myself to go to his funeral. I knew I would not be able to stand it. Even though I know my buddy is dancing down the "Streets of Gold" and locking arms with Jesus, it was too painful for me. Mrs. Woods sent me the program of his home-going worship service, and I could not even open the envelope for a week. When I finally did open it, there was his picture on the center of the page. I held the program against my chest and wept uncontrollably. I don't have many close friends. Losing him really hurt deeply. I think of him so often even now, eight years later, because of the fun times I spent with Mrs. Woods and him. As I write this portion of the book, it is the anniversary of his passing. I felt led to call Mrs. Woods and share this portion with her. Again, Mrs. Woods and I laughed as we reflected, but I also fought back tears though my smile thinking of the great times I had with my friend. What a blessing it will be when we meet again at the feet of Jesus.

Setbacks and Scars along the Way

I grew up hearing people say, "If plan *A* doesn't work, you have to have a plan *B*. In some cases, you may have to go through the alphabet a few times to get to where you want to go. So much in life can scare you, set you back, and defer your plans, your dreams, and your hopes. Setbacks, delays, side steps, inconveniences, sabotages, ambushes, derailments, and even attempted assassinations of your dreams and hopes can and will happen every day, and they will come from the most unlikely places.

I must say that as much as I would love to expose every satanic demon that has ever hurt me, either of my children, my sister, or any member of my church or family, I know that would not be Christlike, even though they have done horrific things. God would get no glory in that at all. The beauty of knowing the Lord is that when you give a problem over to the Lord, you are free to move on. God will deal with demons, according to Galatians 5:10. "I have confidence in you through the Lord, that ye will be none otherwise minded: But he that troubleth you shall bear His judgment, whosoever he be."

I will never mention any of them in any way in my writing. I will not give the devil an audience. In our society, we give too much of an audience to inappropriate behavior and actions in the news. I think that's wrong. My mother had a saying, "Fools' names and fools' faces are always seen in public places." We see that in graffiti and when the news media highlight people who commit horrible offenses. The smaller the caption, the less notoriety those types will get. The less often you call their names, the more you ignore them, the less of a stronghold they will have over your life if you surrender them over to the Lord for Him to deal with. Remember my family rule: the way the adult (in this case, God) deals with those who misbehave is not your business. You just remain free in Christ and focus on the positive things He is doing and has done for you. There are many wonderful

REV. WALTER A. JACKSON III

people in the world who are affirming, uplifting, and positive. Don't waste time on the monsters and demons.

Another reason I will not mention some of them is that I take seriously the Baptist Church covenant that prohibits "needlessly exposing the infirmities of others." There are people in churches who are sometimes act inappropriately—tattling, gossiping, spreading rumors, slandering, sending hate mail, and the like. These things are, of course, sinful. Churchgoers are not perfect, and not all of them are saved. To expose them, as some do, could hinder an opportunity to reach them with the gospel of Jesus Christ. The goal of every Christian should and *must* be to reach, not to destroy. If they refuse to grow, let Jesus deal with them. It is not your business or place. Your job is to pray for them.

There will be setbacks in your life. Sometimes they take your breath away and leave you gasping for air. Some of them leave deep scars that take years to heal. One day, I was so uptight about some malicious and vindictive things that had happened to me that I went as far as to anoint the very street that certain monsters lived on and their places of employment, praying that God would send hungry she bears—or even male grizzlies—with very sharp nails and teeth their way. I wanted God to fix them good. What happened, though, was that God instead showed me how I was allowing their behavior and actions to keep me in bondage, thus allowing them to have a stronghold on my life. I knew I needed to get those demonic forces and festering anger out of my head. It was affecting my health, my appetite, and even keeping me from the things that gave me peace. I went to church late one night and sat in a pew praying. Before I knew it, I was kneeling down in the aisle, and then I was lying facedown on the floor in front of the communion table, praying and crying out to God. I hear very clearly the words of Galatians 5:10 "I have confidence in you through the Lord, that ye will be none otherwise minded: but he that troubleth you shall bear his judgment, whosoever he be".

I got up, sat on the pew, and read that verse. The tears began to flow. Alone, just the Lord and me, I got peace. It was not my business how He was going to handle the situations with the monsters in my life. I just needed to keep my focus on Him. I can't describe the peace that came over me as He ministered to me that night. All I know is that I began to heal that night. No, I won't be seeking out any of those hurtful people to join hands and run down the street singing, "Kumbaya." That is not going to happen. However, I can move on and pray that they never get to hurt others.

Sometimes, your setbacks may be dreams that someone crushed or self-esteem that has been beaten down by abuse or bullying. Whatever it is, you must tell them, "In Jesus's name, I will not be bullied, abused, beaten down, trampled on, intimidated, or controlled by your gossip ever again!"

There is a powerful moment in a Tyler Perry movie when an abused women stands up to her extremely abusive fiancé. Aunt Madea tells the woman that there are grits on the stove, and they are very hot, and her fiancé looks hungry. As Madea leaves the house, we hear the man scream and the sound of a frying pan contacting his head. "The game of grit ball" has been played, and the abused woman has just been set free.

Of course, we don't have to go to those extremes, but the point is that we must never let the monster behavior of Satan's demons keep us from being all that God says we are to be. Turn your setbacks in to stepping stones of faith. Each one that you overcome is a victory to the glory of God. Trust me when I tell you that it can be done in a Godly manner. It may take time for the scars to heal, but if you can keep your focus on Christ, the healing will take place.

The friends I have remained in contact with the longest are from my college days. Rev. Dr. Betty Lancaster Short and her late husband, Bishop Steven N. Short, play a crucial part in helping me really become free in Christ to experience how wonderful walking with Christ can be. I would sometimes call them or visit, and we would sit for hours discussing the things of the Lord. They introduced me to of my closest friends, Dr. Earl Beeks. Earl is a pediatrician and his wife, Esther Beeks, is a dentist. Though we live miles apart, we seem to know in the spirit when to call each other and pray for each other. That friendship has lasted forty years.

God uses many different ways to reach you with the encouragement you need to pull through. Not very long ago, my dear friend Pastor David Housholder, whom I met at a Promise Keepers event for pastors in Atlanta, called me as a result of his prayer time. I had been dealing with some difficult church issues. God had just done a miracle in that situation. Feeling battle weary and a little posttraumatic stress shell shocked, I was sitting in my backyard with my two loyal Labrador retrievers competing for my attention when my cell phone rang. It was Dave. He told me that he had just been praying, and God had given him a word for me. Now, there are only a few people who could tell me that without me telling them to go back and check, Dave is one of them. I was all ears. I was about to get something I needed from God through my West Coast brother in Christ, pastor, and friend. He told me that God had told him to call me and encourage me that day. He told me that God had blessed me with a "survivor's spirit." Just as God did in His word when He reminded the Israelites of all He had done for them, God used my brother to remind me of the things God had helped me to survive. We prayed together, and in true "Walter form," I had my "weeping prophet moment."

We have had other conversations since then, but that one gave me a surge of strength in Christ that I will always remember. I reflected on how we met by chance, walking through the Atlanta Stadium trying to find the room where choir auditions for the next day's event would be held. He followed me because he thought I knew where I was going. I told him that I was just as lost as he was. Yet we found the room. I thought of how God orchestrated that we would both be chosen for the choir and that because of our heights, ended up standing next to each other on the stage. When the Holy Spirit fell on the stadium and thousands of pastors erupted into spontaneous worship and praise at the end of the song "Let the Walls Come Down," the choir was also swept into "the praise zone." There we were, two total strangers who had met by chance the night before, a midwesterner of Scandinavian descent and an easterner of African, Powhatan Indian, and English blood and a descendant of slaves were drawn into a whirlwind of praise and tears as "the walls came down." Nineteen years later, he and his wife, Wendy, are two of my closest friends, though we live on opposite sides of the country. God used my friend to encourage me and renew my strength.

A chance meeting with Michael Adams and Connie Adams opened doors for healing from more setbacks and monsters. Mike and I met on a commuter train because I was wearing a Promise Keepers hat that I had gotten in Atlanta. Mike went with me to a Promise Keepers event in Washington, DC, and later, along with his wife, Connie, sponsored me in a short course on Christianity that played a tremendous part in healing me from setbacks and scars. I count them as part of my family. It was a blessing for me to get an opportunity to introduce Mike and Connie to Dave and Wendy. They, too, are now good friends, and we all keep in contact with each other.

Sometimes you have setbacks because of emotional trauma. You can become a prisoner to your own thoughts and fears. I believe that I read in one of the books in Merlin R. Carothers's Prison to Praise series that the opposite of faith is fear. Fear is the devil's playground in your mind. That is the only way he can do anything to you. Some of the things that have happened to us scare us terribly. We experience deaths, sicknesses, accidents, and catastrophic events. These are all things that can cause setbacks in your aspirations, dreams, and goals. Many people witnessed and experienced September 11, 2001, better known as 9/11. Depending on who you are; where you were that day; and whether you had a connection to anyone at the Twin Towers, at the Pentagon, on the flight that went down in Pennsylvania, or you watched the disaster unfold on television, it did something to you. It left you different. Some took drinking, and others quit drinking. Some became bitter and filled with hatred for anyone who looks as if he or she is of the same ethnic group or religion as the terrorists. New racist words emerged. Some people wrote songs. Others wrote books. Others took a different approach and turned it into a time to reflect that we don't know what a day will bring. We need to cherish every day we have with each other. Others just plain stopped taking life for granted and decided to do something positive with their lives. It boils down to choices. You can choose to let your setbacks make you stronger, or you can choose to let them kill you.

We all have our baggage. How we handle it will determine how well we survive. For a number of years, I was spiritual director for a group that does a short course in Christianity. The group used to do a very powerful Communion service. Sue Himmelwright, who has a wonderful ministry of clowning, did a skit for this Communion on "baggage." She portrayed very sad woman carrying a heavy bag full of painful things, but before she could part with it, Jesus had to help her empty her bag. That is what He has to do for each one of us. (I am not telling you the whole skit, just in case you get to see this wonderful performance. I have not been the same since. I, the weeping prophet, was a big ball of mush.

God wants all your baggage, no matter who or what the baggage is. He will deal with it and begin to heal you so that you can be free in Him. It makes no difference whether that baggage is the perverted police officer who sexually abused a neighbor's five-year-old and his own sister and later took his own life, or the crack addict who robbed you, or the gossiper, or the abusive spouse, or the anonymous letter writer who sent venomous hate mail, or the church member who disrespected or undermined a pastor, or the school teacher or employer who hated you because of the color of your skin or your gender. People I know or know of have been hurt by all of these people or situations. Remember, God will deal with them all. How He does that is none of your business. You just need to let Him help you dump the baggage and begin to heal in Jesus's name.

Don't get me wrong; dumping your issues does not happen overnight. It takes time. It takes patience. However, it can and must be done if you are to have peace and freedom in the Lord. I am still dumping baggage, healing from deep wounds inflicted by others, and wounds inflicted on my children. (*If you hurt my children, you have hurt me. I might have trouble acting saved with you then.* Jesus is working on me in those areas, but don't press your luck!)

The things that don't kill you do make you stronger. Sometimes I look back and reflect on the many things that God gave me victory over. When you stop and think about it, you can see just how He has used everything in your life to bring you to the place where you are right now. When the devil tries to use things against you, God has a way of turning those setbacks into testimonies, those defeats into victories, and those enemies into footstools.

Psalm 23:5 says, "Thou preparest a table before me in the presence of mine enemies: thou anointest my head with oil; my cup runneth over."

If God blesses you where no one can see it, there is no testimony. It is important that God blesses you in such a way that your adversaries see you being blessed by Him. It is important that you allow God to bless you in your enemies' sight so that they realize that God defeats their tactics, antics, and deceptions. It is important that you do not become arrogant and prideful in the blessing so that you don't stoop to the enemy's level. Enough things trip me up in life. I don't need to trip and fall over my pride and arrogance. Let someone else do that kind of falling. That is not for me. Besides, pride can cause you to go crazy. Read Daniel 4:30–37 and see how Nebuchadnezzar went crazy because of pride. No, thank you! That is not something I want to experience. We all need to know that we survive because of the Lord and not of our own doing. Let God prepare your banquet table in the face of your enemies. Sit down with those who love and affirm you and enjoy the meal full of blessings He has for you and for all those who love and trust Him. It is an all-you-can-eat meal of blessings. It's all part of a good spiritual diet, and *God is an excellent cook*!

The Lord has shown me some wonderful things in my life—even through some of the most horrific experiences. I know that before

He calls me home, there will be more scars and setbacks. I am rally-
ing from some even now. However, the beauty of it all is that I shud-
der to think what it would be like if I did not know Him. When I told
my grandma Graham in a letter in 1970 that God had called me to
preach, thus fulfilling the prophetic words she had spoken over me
seventeen years earlier, she wrote back expressing her joy and her an-
ticipation of being present for my initial sermon at Nineteenth Street
Baptist Church. She quoted John 16:33, which says, "These things I
have spoken unto you, that in me ye might have peace. In the world
ye shall have tribulation: but be of good cheer; I have overcome the
world."

Grandma Graham was there that Sunday August 30, 1970, sitting next to Aunt Belle in the second row, wiping the tears from her
eyes with her lace handkerchief. As I stood up to deliver the message,
"The Stick God Gave You," she shouted, "Let God use you, son!" Then
she buried her face in her handkerchief and let the tears fall.

Aunt Belle shouted, "Have mercy!" And then she fainted.

Forty-four years later, having now been pastor at my current
church for thirty-four of those years after three years at another
church, I understand all too well the encouragement Grandma was
giving me. I couldn't see it all then, but I see it very clearly now. When
I experience setbacks or feel discouraged and battle weary, I think of
those nights doing homework—being so tired I could barely keep my
eyes open and even nodding off at times. I hear her encouraging me,
saying, "Keep at it, son. Keep at it!" That makes me want to "stay on
the rock (Christ) just a little while longer" because "I believe I'll run
on and see what the end is going to be!"

3

THE LORD IS IN HIS HOLY TEMPLE

"The Lord is in his holy temple: let all the earth keep silent before him." These words from Habakkuk 2:20 were inscribed over the archway above the choir loft and pulpit of the old Nineteenth Street Baptist Church. For the first twenty-four years of my life and the last twenty-four years that the church was at the corner of Nineteenth and I Streets NW before moving to Sixteenth and Buchannan Streets NW, that phrase dominated my life. When I walked into the church even before I knew how to read, I knew those words. This was more powerful than Miss Martha H. Winston's rule about no gum chewing. It was more powerful than the teaching about respecting adults. These words declared, proclaimed, and mandated that you were entering the place where God Himself was present, and you were to respect, honor, worship, and adore Him in His house.

In His house, you had to go by His rules. I had visions, as a child, of God opening a trap door in heaven that allowed Him to stick His face in and look at us in church, sitting there in worship. I used to envision His face filling the entire ceiling of the sanctuary as He kept a close eye on each of us in His house. If that was not enough, on the I Street side of the balcony over the vestibule doors, where the Beasley family sat, there was a picture representing Jesus knocking at a door. ("Behold I stand at the door and knock. If any man hear and open,

I will come in and sup with him and he with Me.") Hanging over the vestibule doors on the Pennsylvania Avenue side, near the now infamous Jackson pews, was a picture representing Jesus holding a lamb. ("I am the Good Shepherd.") Those two phrases from scripture, I later learned, were what the pictures were to represent.

Each stained-glass window in the church depicted a different passage of scripture. Churches with stained-glass windows need to know, if they do not, where the concept of the pictures came from. They date back to the Middle Ages, before the general population could read. The pictures on the windows helped to teach the story of the gospel of Jesus Christ. When I see churches that have stained glass, and the picture is the same in all of the windows, I know that the members do not know the purpose of them.

Even before my salvation experience, I would ask my parents, grandparents, aunts, and uncles about the pictures. I realize now that that was a witness to me even then. They seemed to be all over the church back then. Each week in Sunday school, we got pictures that we pasted in scrapbooks. They also told us the gospel story. I remember vividly my mother helping me put pictures in a red-covered scrapbook with black pages and talking to me about the pictures. It was like getting a new baseball card each week. I would love to find a series like that now. Everywhere I looked, there were picture stories that told me about the one who would, one day, be my savior and my friend.

This Family Goes to Church!

Growing up in the tribal clan of Jackson/Graham/Grant, you learned that all three of those family branches had a deep connection to worship. It was and still is a big part of who we are as a family. The matriarchs and patriarchs of all three branches of the family set the tone. They were like the ones who blew the shofar in Israel to call the twelve tribes to worship. They went to church and were leaders in their respective churches—Nineteenth Street Baptist, Mount Olive

Baptist, and Mount Zion Baptist—and we, the rest of their tribal clan, followed. There was no option. There was no challenge.

Once and *only* once, that lesson was taught to me, and it never had to be taught again. It was also, I believe, when the concepts of stereo and surround sound were invented, in early1954. No matter what the history of audio technology may tell you, my parents invented those concepts one Sunday in the early evening.

We had gotten out of church around noon. We had dinner with Grandma and Granddaddy Jackson and then went for a ride in the country in our 1949 Mercury. I was sitting up front between my mother and my father. Of course, we still had our church clothes on. My mother liked frozen custard, so we stopped and got frozen custard. Ice cream and anything that runs on rails are my drugs of choice, even to this day. Upon finishing our treats and me getting "unsticky," Daddy started driving again. I asked, "Where're we going now?"

"We're going back to church" was the reply. Now, three-year-olds are sometimes known to have momentary "terrible-two" memory lapses. My brain somehow disengaged. I don't know how. Maybe the ice cream had frozen a brain cell or two, but in true "I am three years old and have lost my mind" form, I blurted distinctly, defiantly, and irreverently, "I don't want to go to no old church!"

It was in the early days of 1954, before my beloved sister, Cynthia, was born and before stereo and surround sound were invented. But the back of my mother's left hand somehow was introduced to the right side of my mouth just as my father's right hand had fellowship with the left side of my mouth.

My right ear heard the sound, and my left ear heard the sound. It was not one of those slaps that would knock you for a row of ash cans, but it was enough of a tap to reconnect the synapses of my brain and free me from my defiant moment. At that same time, my parents said in unison the words that still ring in my ears distinctly, loudly, slowly, and with harmonic resolve, *This family goes to church!* The case was closed, and the "amen" was said to that behavior. I don't remember ever talking back to my parents again. Those stereo backhands and the surround sound in my ears of what we do as a family have never left me. My father has a phrase that he sometimes says, the sanctified version of which is, "You're not going to rub my backside but one time with a wire brush. It won't happen a second time." That lesson, like many others, I only had to be taught but once. That once was enough for me.

My sister, Cynthia, and I were like most siblings. As children, we were as different as night and day. I was the *Little House on the Prairie* child, compliant to a fault. Cynthia, on the other hand, was like *Star Trek*; she was a maverick, bold, adventurous, daring, and on the edge. She would "boldly go where no one has gone before."

If you told me to sit in a chair on the front porch and not to move, I would be there in that same spot in that chair until the rapture of the church. If you told Cynthia to sit in the chair, she would interpret that to mean that as long as the chair was making contact with her rear end, she was complying. She has the personality type that would allow her to pick up the chair and move about the room, house, or neighborhood holding the chair against her rear end. If someone said something to her, she would let the chair rest on all four legs and say, "But I am still in the chair." Yes, this family goes to church!

Cynthia paid attention to the lessons learned in Sunday school and church. We both learned the sacred text but came away with different exegeses and hermeneutic understandings of God's word. She understood the Golden Rule, but her interpretation was "Do unto others just like or before they do unto you."

One time, a girl threatened to fight Cynthia on the way home from school. Cynthia had ignored this girl, who had a little gang of fifth graders following her. The girl slapped Cynthia and then took off her glasses so she and her friends could really take Cynthia on. I am not sure what went through Cynthia's mind. Maybe she had done the math and figured that if she turned the other cheek, there might be more slaps than she had cheeks to turn. At any rate, Cynthia had a "laying on of hands service" on that girl that was so powerful it caused her ladies-in-waiting to flee. Cynthia knocked the girl to the ground as though she had been slain in the spirit. Even the girl's older brother, who was my age, ran off under Cynthia's power. Cynthia had put something on her that Clorox would have to take off—along with two black eyes.

Later, the girl's parents called about the incident. They wondered why Cynthia had attacked their poor, defenseless daughter and given her two black eyes. The girl's father told my dad, "How dare she hit a girl with glasses!"

My father said, "So, I have to pay for a pair of glasses?"

"No, her glasses are not broken," he responded.

My dad then said, "I am having trouble understanding how your daughter has two black eyes, no cuts on her face from broken frames, and the glasses are not broken."

There was a long pause. Then the girl's father said, "Mr. Jackson, let me ask a few more questions on my end and call you back. A few minutes later, he called back and told my father, "I think I have a better picture of what happened. My daughter instigated the fight and had some girls with her to back her up. The girls left when my daughter took off her glasses so they would not get broken. It also appears that I have to deal with my son for lying and saying that your daughter jumped his sister when he was one of the instigators."

Grace and mercy saved Cynthia from the wrath of my mother and father that night. I believe she was also saved by reminding our parents that she was only doing what she had been taught in church. She said, "Daddy, I was just doing what the Bible said. I had turned one cheek so she couldn't slap the other one."

At that moment, my father looked at my mother and shook his head. Momma looked shocked. Grandma looked up from her Bible and laughed. We all laughed. Cynthia was trying to understand the humor of what the Bible had taught her. At least her interpretation had led her to hold it as gospel truth. After all, this family goes to church! Cynthia meant to put it into practice in her life to the best of her understanding. I often laugh about that incident with Rev.

Cynthia Jackson Swann—my dear, beloved sister and friend. And we still go to church!

That was not the first time Cynthia had practiced her version of "laying on of hands." When she was in the second grade, a little girl with blond hair, who was also a second grader, decided to call Cynthia a name. She didn't call her just any name. She used the worst insult that you can call any person of color. She dropped the *n* word on Cynthia.

Cynthia didn't even know what the word meant. All she knew was that this little girl had called her a name. Cynthia had a blue vinyl-covered lunch box with a thermos in it. She hit that little girl on the head with that lunch box. The girl said it again, and Cynthia hit her again. Again, the girl said it, and again, Cynthia hit her—three of four times—until the little girl decided to remove that word from her vocabulary, at least in Cynthia's presence. I was on safety patrol then, and I remember trying to get her to stop hitting the girl. The next day, she and the little girl were playing together on the playground. The following Sunday in Sunday school, we sang,

> Jesus loves the little children,
> All the children of the world.
> Red and yellow, black, and white,
> All are precious in His sight.
> Jesus loves the little children of the world.

As we sang it, I had visions of all sorts of children holding hands and skipping across a school playground carrying little blue-vinyl lunch boxes, as Cynthia led the way.

The Tribal Leaders Set the Tone

As I mentioned, the matriarchs and patriarchs set the tone for the family in many areas. Worship was the most important area where the tone was set for us all. They were the role models in how to govern yourself in your everyday life, how to interact with others, how to organize your life, how to act in public, and most importantly, how to worship.

Nana had a certain organization to her life that she did not deviate from until her health began to fail and she became what used to be called "senile." Now we call it Alzheimer's disease or dementia. Nana ran her home on a folktale schedule:

- Monday was wash day.
- Tuesday was ironing day.
- Wednesday was mending day.
- Thursday was cleaning day.
- Friday was shopping day.
- Saturday was cooking day.
- Sunday was the Lord's day.

You could walk by her house and know what day it was by what she was doing. On Sunday morning, she would be standing on her front porch, waiting for my grandfather (her son) to drive around the corner to pick her up for Sunday school and church at Metropolitan Baptist. After picking her up, he would drive the ten blocks to the apartment we occupied before we bought our first home and pick me up for Sunday school. My parents would come later.

Nana had her morning time for Bible reading and prayer before she did her chores. Then she would call her daughter-in-law, Grandma Jackson, for a brief chat. Nana sometimes needed me to walk to the corner store and pick something up for her to tide her over until she did her marketing on Friday. On Fridays, she, like Grandma Jackson, would walk to the meat market and fish market. Granddaddy Jackson would go to the A&P grocery store for the rest of what was needed for his house and his mother's house.

The meat and fish market was interesting because the fresh fish were laid out on ice, and you picked out what you wanted. The attendant would put it on the scale and then wrap it in brown paper and tie it with string. Sides of cows and hogs were hanging on meat hooks, and the butcher would cut the cuts of meat you wanted to your specifications. You walked through an area filled with cages of live chickens, and you picked the birds you wanted for your Sunday dinner. They were killed and defeathered while you waited. It would be the same for turkeys at Thanksgiving and Christmas. Food tasted so much better then.

After Granddaddy Jackson retired from the Government Printing Office and started driving for several funeral homes, he had a morning routine. After he bathed, shaved, and dressed except for his shirt and tie, he would sit in a chair by his bedroom window and read his Bible. The light would be on in the bedroom, but he always sat in such a way that the morning sunlight would catch the pages of the Bible. If you wanted to ask him a question or say something to him, Grandma Jackson would say, "Children, don't bother Granddaddy. He's reading his Bible." Sometimes I would just stand there and watch him. He would be ever so still and quiet. It would seem like the sun was reflecting off the page, onto his face, causing his face to radiate with brightness. Oh, God! How I miss those moments! Even now, I can see him ever so clearly. Then he would tenderly close that tattered and worn Bible. While still holding it with one hand, he would cover his eyes with his other hand, and for a brief moment, he would silently pray. His lips would move, but there was not a sound to be heard.

I knew that something sacred and solemn was taking place. "The Lord was in His holy temple" (my granddaddy), and he had become silent in God's presence. He would put on his shirt and tie only after these few moments alone in the presence of God. Without ever saying a word to me about it, he taught me how important and how special it is to have your time with God in meditation, study, prayer, and reflection.

I would watch him put on his black suit jacket, and as he would start down the stairs and head out the door, Grandma would say, "Jackson, do you have your face?" (She meant his chauffeur's license.)

We would echo, "Granddaddy, do you have your face?" He would look at us, point to his chin, and say with a smile, "It's right here."

I have loved trains since I was three years old. However, I did not know there was a hymn about trains until I heard Grandma Jackson singing it as she was bouncing my sister on her knee as an infant. My thought then was, Wow! They even have trains running in heaven! When I hear that song now, I think of the first time I heard it coming from her lips. It's too bad some of those hymns are not sung as they once were. A lot of wonderful worship heritage is being thrown away as outdated and antiquated. Listening to Grandma, who was not a member of the choir and did not sing solos like her son did, I learned to keep a song in my heart at all times. She taught me to come into God's presence with singing.

Years later, my daughter and my son would tell me at times (even in public), "Dad, you're humming again!" I was in the grocery store once, standing in line, and a woman behind me started harmonizing with me. I had not realized that I was humming (as usual). She said, "I am sorry. I couldn't help it. You were sounding so good. I hadn't heard that song in years. I just wanted to join in with you."

I laughed and told her it was OK. "I was just remembering my grandmother, who used to hum every so often while she was doing her work around the house. What was I humming?"

She said, "Life Is Like a Mountain Railroad."

"That is what she used to hum," I said. A chill went up my spine as I realized I had gone into God's presence with singing in the grocery store, and for a brief moment, someone else had gone there with me.

Grandma Graham, as I mention earlier, had a spiritual presence that commanded you to join her in a place of worship—or at least take notice. Her Bible was her constant companion and friend. She rarely missed church. Worship was as important for her as breathing was. She would allow God's presence to soak into her in such a way that several days after Sunday, she was still going over the key points of a sermon in her mind.

When she lived with us, we were not allowed to go downstairs on Christmas Day and open any presents until Momma and Daddy woke up. That always seemed like an eternity. Then, before we touched anything under the tree, we had to have family prayer and sing a verse and the chorus of a hymn. It was usually "Silent Night," "O Come All Ye Faithful," or "Jesus the Light of the World." Grandma Graham would usually break down and cry. Then, for a moment or two, you wouldn't feel like touching anything.

One Christmas, Cynthia and I were sitting on the top stair outside our bedrooms, smelling the scent of the Christmas tree, which always seemed so much more intense on Christmas morning. We were whispering and discussing what we thought might be under the tree and how long it was going to take our exhausted parents to wake up. (You know, they had wait up to let "Mr. Claus" in, since we had no chimney. At least that was the story we were told. However, I am not going to go there!)

As Cynthia and I were having this discussion, we did not realize that Grandma Graham, who we thought was sleeping, was listening to every word. Cynthia said, "We could die of heart attacks waiting for them to wake up, and you know we have to pray and sing before we open anything. I don't think I can make it, Walter!"

Grandma burst out laughing, got up, and went to my parents' bedroom door. "Betty, Walter, you all come pray so we can let these children go downstairs so they don't have heart attacks."

We prayed at the top of the stairs and had no song that year. Grandma, Momma, and Daddy were laughing too hard at my sister and me, who went down the steps like an express train named the Christmas Limited. I learned from that experience that even in worship, sometimes there is humor. After all, after everything God created, He said, "That's good." Therefore a little humor in worship is good too.

Grandma continued to call the family to worship. She blew her shofar at Christmas by calling us to prayer. Granddaddy Jackson blew his shofar by expecting his grown children and his grandchildren to be in church. He would ask where you were if you did not show up. Grandma Jackson blew her shofar during the week when we stayed with her, prior to Grandma Graham moving in with us, by making sure we said grace before each meal and our prayers at nap time.

The thing I learned from my great-grandmother, Aunt Belle, my grandparents, and my parents is how to organize your life to get things done. (I am still working at gaining mastery of that.) In their homes, certain things were done on certain days and at certain times. No matter whose house we were in, dinner was at a set time, and we ate together as a family. Everyone sat at the table at the same time for a family meal. Meals were well planned, balanced, and healthy. You didn't snack too close to dinner because it would "spoil your dinner." Nothing was wasted. Usually there was enough cooked on Sunday that there were leftovers for Monday. A turkey from Thanksgiving usually ended up being served for a couple of days. You would see that turkey in turkey soup, turkey with noodles, creamed turkey over toast or rice, turkey croquettes, turkey salad, and turkey sandwiches for lunch. The same would be done with chicken. Ham would show up as ham sandwiches for lunch, ham salad, ham in macaroni and cheese with diced tomatoes, and ham and eggs for breakfast. The bone, with what meat was left on it, would end up in great northern beans, dried lima beans, black-eyed peas, split-pea soup, or pinto beans, all of which would be served with corn bread. You just didn't see food thrown away.

When we got an ice cream freezer, my mother experimented with different recipes for ice cream. Ice cream is still my drug of choice—vanilla, cherry vanilla, peach, and pineapple. I also like certain orange sherbets. My mother made some orange sherbet that I thought was awful. The recipe called for grated orange peels. The flavor was OK, but the orange peels were not something my taste buds found pleasurable. I don't think anyone else's did, either. I think that sherbet sat in the deep freeze for a long time. It would have been a candidate for freezer burn if it had not been for Grandma Graham.

Grandma Graham made the best pound cakes and peach cobblers. I came home from school for lunch one day to a wonderful-smelling pound cake in the oven. She gave me a big slice of it. It was so good that I begged her for a slice to eat as I walked back to school. Not saying a word, she just smiled and gave me another big hunk of that cake. It had a slightly different flavor than her usual pound cakes, and it had an orange hue. It was so tender and so sweet.

For dessert that evening, there was a brand-new pound cake and the other half of the one that I sampled at lunchtime. We sat there after dinner and finished off one and a half pound cakes. "Grandma," I said. "When are you going to make another pound cake like that? It was so good!"

She smiled and said, "As soon as your mother makes some more of that sherbet you all didn't like, I'll make another one." We laughed so hard that I was in tears. She had used that grated orange-peel sherbet for the pound cakes instead of milk. She was determined not to waste it. She had a way of taking the cream of wheat I didn't eat in the morning and concealing it in the homemade soup she'd make me for lunch. The soup would taste good, though the cream of wheat at breakfast would make me want to gag.

So, there were life lessons learned about not wasting valuable resources. Use everything you have for a good purpose. Grandma Jackson used to say, "Waste not, want not." My grandparents had raised my parents during the Great Depression. They had experience rationing during World War II. They were not so sure that those hard times would not come back again. If they did, they would know how to make it through. They wanted us to know, too.

They wanted us to know not just how to manage life in general but also in the worship of God. They modeled for us the "best practices of worship." They showed us by example how to respect the house of worship and the shepherd of the flock. They took a very dim view of people who disrespected pastors. I remember overhearing my grandparents discussing a situation in which a person was spreading gossip about a preacher. I remember them agreeing that the gossiper was in sin, and if the preacher was in fact in the wrong, God would deal with him. However, God also would deal with the gossiper for trying to do

God's job. The congregants' job should be to pray for the preacher and stay out of God's business. Their job—and the gossiper's—is to pray for the pastor not tear him or her down. They taught us that you can't take back what you have said or done once you destroy a person.

Rev. W. A. Clark's phrase was, "Be treatin' everybody right because you don't know whose hands you going to fall into." Those words ring so true now. I have seen so many situations where the words of the elders in my life have come true.

The tone was set for my sister, my cousins, and me. We are active in church and have taken our places as the next-in-line patriarchs and matriarchs of the Jackson clan. We are more spread out geographically now. Some are still at Nineteenth Street Baptist; Cynthia is at Mount Bethel Baptist, near Pittsburgh, as an associate minister; and I am at Wainwright Baptist in Charles Town, West Virginia, as pastor. The seeds planted in each of us so long ago, I pray, will sprout up in or children, grandchildren, and great-grandchildren even long after we have gone to join our elders on that "mountain railroad" whose destination is that "blissful shore" called heaven, where we will reign with Jesus forevermore.

What You Learned (Even in Quiet Rebellion)
Did you ever make mental plans when you were a child about things you were or were not going to do as an adult? I made several! I have maintained some of them to this very day and will do so until Jesus calls me home. In my family, you ate whatever was put on your plate. It was not an option to turn your nose up at any food. However, some foods are just not in agreement with the taste buds of some children. There are two breakfast foods that I have absolutely *no* taste for to this day and will *never* again eat. At the top of that list is *oatmeal*! Yes, I know all of the things that oatmeal is supposed to be good for and the health benefits of it. The only thing it is good for in my book is making cookies. Because it is inexpensive and healthy, what do you think one of the regular breakfast foods was at Grandma Jackson's? You guessed it. Oatmeal! Whatever was put in front of Granddaddy

for breakfast was what you got too. He loved oatmeal. You could rest assured that it would be served a couple of times a week. Grandma could doctor it up with cream, peaches, sugar, cherries, or whatever she wanted. I was still going to go to "Gag City" trying to eat it. The stern looks and warnings from Granddaddy didn't change that either. "Boy! Eat your breakfast!" he'd say, sometimes tapping the back of my head with his hand. He had worked too hard to put food on the table for children to waste it. A few times, I sat there staring at it until almost lunchtime.

I mumbled under my breath one time, "When I grow up, I am never eating this stuff again!" I never knew my grandfather could move so fast. That man whirled me out of that chair with one hand, and grabbed his little razor strap, which must have been a hundred years old, with the other. I was wearing short pants. He stung my legs a few times with it and seated me on the sofa. From then on, I made my declarations to myself. I told you I learn quickly. That was a line I never crossed again. They didn't make me eat oatmeal anymore. There would be cornflakes, Rice Krispies or Trix, but no more oatmeal. Cream of wheat and waffles are two other foods that I will not eat. If I eat pancakes, I must have bacon, sausage, or ham with them and maple syrup, not molasses. However, in true Southern form, I'll jump over two government mules and a spotted dog for a bowl of grits with some butter on them!

I made mental notes about what I was not going to do and how different I was going to be when I was grown. I knew I could never mention many of those things aloud because my elders would assume I was being disrespectful. However, as I grew older, I understood why my parents and grandparents wanted to know where I was and whose house I was going to. I understand now why they would get upset if I was not where I told them I would be. It makes sense now that when they told me to be indoors when the streetlights come on, they had a very good reason. There were monsters that lurked in the streets after dark especially—and some that prowled in the daytime. I still have nightmares about a rash of children that went missing around

1958 and were never found. In two cases, decomposing bodies were found. I realize now that that would have devastated my entire family.

I wanted to know where my children were too. I would get upset if I didn't get a phone call letting me know where they were. At sixty-four, I still "report in" to my ninety-year-old father. He is still my dad, and he would still be worried. In the same way, if my sister and I don't hear from him, we worry. It is a matter of respect, love, and concern for the ones you love. If I forget to call him in the morning and call later, I know I am going to hear something like, "I didn't know whether you were lying down there with a tag on your toe or what." Then I know I have some explaining to do.

Back-talking was not an option when I was growing up. I cringe when I hear kids back-talking adults. I have to take a deep breath when it happens to me when I work as a substitute teacher. I just grit my teeth and write discipline referrals. This might be a new day, but respect is still respect. When children ask me my first name at school, I politely smile and say, "Mister."

My way of rebellion was subtle. Nineteenth Street Baptist Church was what was called in some African American circles "a silk-stocking church." The meaning of that (not to be negative) was that it was a church of upper-middle-class African Americans and had a more reserved style of worship. Baptist churches, with each congregation being sovereign—not controlled by a bishop or presiding prelate—can vary in their style of worship from almost Anglican in terms of music, order of service, and style of preaching to near Pentecostal in the flavor of music and style of preaching. There are degrees in between. Nineteenth Street was rather "high order." It was only two blocks from the White House and its members included Dr. Charles Drew and Mercer Ellington, the son of Duke Ellington, along with many other notables in the DC area. We sang hymns the exact way they were written in the hymnbook with no deviation and anthems by Beethoven, Bach, and Handel. I grew up knowing the baritone and bass line of Handel's "Messiah Hallelujah Chorus." My rebellion was in wanting to sing and play gospel music like they sang at Mount

Zion and Mount Olive and like I heard in the storefront churches we sometimes passed on the way to church or on the radio on Sunday mornings.

I wanted to change churches and go where they sang those kinds of songs, and my parent said no. I knew I had to comply. However, I bought all the gospel albums I could get my hands on with my money. When I went to college, I was determined to find a church that had the kind of worship I liked. I even learned to beat a tambourine and play the bongos. That was the way I rebelled. However, God used all of that to reach me and to bring me to where I am in Him. I knew better than to rebel and be disrespectful to my parents because I would also be disrespecting God by doing so.

If I got upset with my parents about something, one thing was not going to happen. I was not going to mouth off at them. I knew better. I would comply and do what they said. I would just get very quiet. Then I would only speak if I were spoken to or asked a question. I also knew that I'd better not display an attitude. In my head, I might be thinking what I wanted to say, but I wouldn't even *think* about verbalizing it in a disrespectful way. They always knew when I was upset with them.

One day, my mother told me, "I know you're in quiet rebellion. Let us know when you are ready to talk about it."

I turned and looked at my dad in shock and surprise.

He said, "Don't look at me; you heard your mother. We know you. You might not like what we have to say, but this is the way it is going to be. I know you're mad enough to cuss, but you won't." They laughed, and I did too. Even in my quiet rebellion, I learned that my parents were looking out for my best interest.

I made mental notes about what type of church I would attend, where I would live, how I would be with my children when I had them, and how different I was going to be from them. However, my values are very much like theirs. My style of worship is not exactly like theirs, but it's very similar with just a little more spice added. Like my dad, I'll do anything in the world for you, but if you cross the line and lose your place in my inner circle, you won't get back in. I will not be mean to you, but you will not get that close again. You are demoted to acquaintance status. Like my mother, I process things, attempt to look at issues from all sides, and try to do well whatever I do. Like my dad, I try to have a good, sidesplitting laugh at least once a day. Grandma Jackson had a saying, "Smile and the world smiles with you, frown and you frown alone." Like both of my parents, I don't like confusion and drama. Life is too short to waste time with that. I especially hate drama at church. I think it really rattles God, too.

As I spoke with Mrs. Woods to ask if she would mind me sharing of my relationship with her and Reverend Woods, she made a statement that rings true. She said, "All you can do is raise your children the best you can and then pray and hope for the best." I believe that is what my parents, aunts, and uncles did for my cousins and me. I remember one time my mother made this statement in a conversation: "We are not perfect, but we are your parents." The same can be said for Christians; we are not perfect, but we are forgiven.

I don't think Cynthia will mind if I tell you that I prayed for seven years for her to be saved and to come to know Christ truly. She was a really tough cookie. She started working as a police officer not long after I started operating Metrobuses in DC. I was also spending a lot of time with my friends in healing and deliverance services. Anointing people with oil, as was done scripturally, is a common practice in some circles. I was determined not to stop praying until I knew my sister was *surely* saved! I had gotten a large bottle of Pompeian olive oil from the local grocery store and prayed over it for anointing for healing and fighting off the wiles of the devil. I also kept the same brand at home for cooking.

A friend had given me the recipe for a rice dish that had shrimp, pepperoni, boned chicken, peas, and saffron sautéed in—of all things—olive oil. I had invited Cynthia by my apartment to try it. As I was preparing it before she arrived, I reached into a kitchen cabinet for my cooking olive oil and discovered that I was out of it. What was I to do? There was no time to go to the store to get more. Then it hit me. I had been anointing my sister's car when she didn't know it to keep her safe. Why not cook the rice dish with the anointed olive oil? It might soften her heart to hear the Lord calling her.

I ran into my bedroom, grabbed the oil off my nightstand, where I kept it next to my Bible, and poured it into the frying pan. "Jesus, as I pour this oil, You touch her heart with every mouthful she eats. In Jesus's name, amen." God has to have a sense of humor. I stood there praying and stirring. A sweet, savory aroma filled the apartment and spread into the hall. When Cynthia came in, we sat down and ate. She raved about how good the dish tasted. We had two helpings apiece. Then she took some in a container for lunch at work.

I don't remember when I told her that I had used the blessed version of the cooking oil to fix the meal. We laugh about it to this day. I tell her that was the meal that caused the truth of Jesus to sink in. I must strongly emphasize that the oil I used was for cooking, not the variety you buy in little bottles in Christian books stores. That oil is not to be consumed. This was cooking oil from a grocery store. Only this bottle of olive oil had been to church and been sanctified! Now Cynthia was too! A year later, I prayed with her to receive Christ.

When the Message Sinks In

At some point, things begin to click. You begin to connect the dots. Rebellion turns into surrender, and things begin to make sense. It doesn't happen all at once. It happens a little at a time. When my grandparents and my parents corrected us about something, they used to say, "One day, you're going to thank me for it." I would think to myself, "*Oh no, I won't.*" The truth of the matter is that the older I get, the more I realize what they said is true. Grandma Graham used to say, "I may be dead and buried, but one day, you are going to remember my words and thank me." Well, Grandma, that day has come! Momma, that day has come! Granddaddy, that day has come! Uncle Louis, Aunt Cinnie, Aunt Katie, Uncle Morris, that day has come! Jesus, give them a big hug for me, please. Let them know that I was listening when they thought I was not. I did hang onto every word that came out of their mouths.

My dad was talking with a neighbor a few weeks ago as he and I sat on his front porch. He was telling the neighbor about the lessons he learned from my grandfather. Then he said that he wasn't sure he had done the best thing for my sister and me because he had tried to make sure we had transportation to school and did not have to go through some of what he'd gone through as a child.

I told him, "Daddy, you didn't realize we were watching you and Momma. We may not have said much, but we were watching. We watched your work ethic and your sacrifices. How do you think I ended up working three jobs? I got that work ethic from you." He just smiled.

There comes a time when the lessons of your youth sink into your soul and become a part of who you are. Knowledge does you no good unless you can take ownership of it and apply it to your life in some way. If there is no way to apply what you have learned and internalize it so that it can become second nature to you, you haven't learned anything. It's just facts and words.

I used to be fascinated by the stories my great-grandmother, great-great aunt, and my grandparents would tell of their childhoods. While other children didn't want to take time to listen to the stories of the old people in their families, I was fascinated by the stories of mine. Their lives seemed so rich. Their struggles seemed so daunting. Their courage was so inspiring. I wonder if the stories of my life will be as inspirational to my children and grandchildren.

I remember once hearing my mother say that she worried because my cousins would be outside playing when we went to Youngstown, and I would be sitting and listening to Grandma's stories. She said she noticed that I would hang on every word as it came out of her mouth. I was fascinated that her mother had given birth to nineteen children and had raised nine that lived. She told of how her father had been her first schoolteacher. She told of how her grandfather, Jack Myree, had been a preacher, though he was born in slavery. I learned that her father was born five years after the end of slavery. I learned that her mother had become ill, and Grandma had to stop school at the end of eighth grade to take care of her younger brothers and sisters.

When all the lessons you learned as a child begin to make sense and have reason, you can begin to live. When the spiritual truths of Christ that you were taught become a part of your being and not just formality and ritual, then the Lord can begin to reside in your soul and spirit. You then can begin to "connect the dots" of your knowledge with your spiritual truths. Those seeds that were planted so long ago with every song that you were taught and every Bible verse you learned helped to bring you to the place where you are in Christ, if you now know Him. However, that can only take place if your heart is open to accept the things that God has laid out before you through others and through His word.

Two verses come to my mind that helped this ring true for me. Proverbs 22:6 says, "Train up a child in the way he should go: and when he is old, he will not depart from it." 2 Timothy 2:15 says, "Study to shew (show) thyself approved unto God, a workman that needeth not to be ashamed, rightly dividing the word of truth." The problem with many church people is that those truths never make the transition from head to heart. When that happens, they are either legalistic or ritualistic, but they are not relational. No dots are ever connected in their souls. These people may be able to rattle off Bible verses, but they never apply them to their lives. They are just noisy words of, as I Corinthians 13 puts it, "a sounding brass and a tinkling cymbal."

I know there are probably many who would take issue with some of what I hold true and believe. That is OK. We each should be convinced in our own minds and in the convictions of our hearts, based on our understanding of God's word. I thank God that He has allowed me to grow and transition from a place of bondage to a place of freedom in Him because He has allowed me to continue to grow through His word. Some of the things I now hold as truth are due to my continuing study of God's word, just as I saw my grandparents and great-grandmother and parents do. I learned to highlight in my study Bible. I learned to take notes and make notes from my mother, who made a habit of it and cross-referenced verses in the margins of her Bible. No, I don't have all the answers, and to borrow a school system phrase, I am "a lifelong learner" of God's word. Like Grandma Graham and Granddaddy Jackson, I have learned to meditate on God's word. Sometimes I will think about one verse or passage of scripture all day and ponder its meaning for me that day. I attempt to glean from that verse as much as I can. I do not wasting anything—just like those meals that were cooked when I was growing up. I want to get everything I can out of each session I have in God's word. Even the drippings that are left over are used to make gravy. That's when you are singing a hymn like Grandma Jackson would hum.

Grandma Graham, Granddaddy Jackson, and Nana spent time each day in their Bibles, and Grandma Jackson hummed hymns while she worked because they had powerful relationships with Christ! They showed me by their example how to enter into the holy temple of the Lord's presence through His word and through song. They passed that knowledge on to me by example and by living it out before me. The seeds of those relationships they had with Christ would one day take root in my soul and spirit. Yes, my mother was right; I hung on every word that came from Grandma Graham's mouth as gospel truth and the things that the other family elders did as mandates on how to enter into God's presence. Other times I just sit in silence and reflect. I reflect in the temple of His presence in sweet silence and surrender.

Everything in life should be a teachable moment and a knowledge-gaining moment. What did I learn from all those people in my family I have mentioned? I learned that my life had value to them. They had high hopes for me. They valued me. They loved me. What have I learned from my friendships that have lasted, in some cases, forty years? Those friends and I walk together as friends because we speak into each other's lives the oracles of God that encourage, affirm, and edify each of us in Christ and in our fellowship and friendship. Those are not things that one can ever take for granted or take casually or lightly. Not everyone you know can or will be included in such a relational cadre. Those relationships take years to nurture, grow, and affirm. Through them, a level of trust is established because of the foundation in Christ's love.

Sometimes I can almost hear God audibly asking me the question that parents sometimes ask their children, "So what have you learned from this lesson so far?"

"Well, God, I have learned that there is so much that I have yet to learn. The more I think I know about You, the more, I realize, there is yet to know. I am still discovering the 'me' Your Son died for, but I am glad He did. You must really love me, God. You know, God, You used a whole lot of situations, people, and stuff to get me to this place, huh? God, I think I am starting to get it now. It is beginning to make sense. God, if You keep talking, and I know You will, I'll keep listening."

I know He will ask me that question again and again and again. Every time I go to another level, there will be some new truth, some new revelation, and some new insight into His word that will have to sink in. However, when it does sink in, I will have to internalize it and take ownership of it in order to grow. That is the beauty of knowing Him Who died for me. That is the joy of being in His holy temple.

4

THE CALL TO PREACH THE GOSPEL

Nothing is more humbling, fulfilling, and rewarding than a call to preach the gospel of Jesus Christ. Some would say my call might have been the result of a strict church upbringing. Others may say they could see it coming, as did my grandma Graham. Later, many would say they knew very early that there was an anointing and a call on my life. Aunt Cinnie said I was always a serious child. My mother used to say that I was born old.

A lot had led up to God calling me into ministry. I resisted and ran the other way. I wanted to design buildings because I loved to draw. It was also my heart's desire to be a railroad engineer. In the 1950s and early 1960s, that career was not open to African Americans. You could be a Pullman porter or, as my uncle Sidney was, a cook on the Baltimore and Ohio Railroad—he often worked on the premier train the Capitol Limited, which ran from Washington, DC, to Chicago. I also wanted to be a streetcar motorman, but Washington, DC, got rid of streetcars, as ordered by Congress, in 1962. (Now after fifty years, what the city never should have gotten rid of is returning, and I live out that childhood dream by operating them at three streetcar museums.)

At the age of sixteen, I sang with the Cathedral Choir of the Nineteenth Street Baptist Church, which was a gospel choir. I was the youngest member of the choir. I took some ribbing from some of the kids my age, who sang with the teenage choir group. I wanted to sing gospel music. That was the music that was drawing me. This was, as I mentioned, my form of quiet rebellion. The Cathedral Choir itself was revolutionary for the church. My singing in that choir was also revolutionary. The rest of the choir members were in their twenties and thirties. I was sixteen.

Reverend Moore had a preaching engagement at a church in New York City. The Cathedral Choir accompanied him. My parents drove my sister and me to New York. I sang with the group. There was something different about Reverend Moore's sermon that day. He mentioned that when the Lord reaches out for you and draws you to Him and calls you by name, you must answer. It was as though he was speaking directly to me, even though I was in the choir stand behind him. As we sang the recessional hymn, which was a gospel selection called "God Be With You," I felt as though I was floating in God's presence. I felt Him with me. "This can't be," I thought. "I am just sixteen. Why me?"

We visited a cousin of my mother's on Long Island after church. All the way back to DC that evening, I heard that song over and over in my head. "God be with you. God be with you. God be with you, till we meet again. Just keep on working for the master. He'll be with you ever after. God be with you till we meet again." That night and every night for three months, I dreamed I was preaching to a congregation, walking the aisles, holding a Bible open, and pouring every bit of energy I had into telling the congregation how Christ would be with them as a choir sang "God Be With You" in the background. I would always wake myself up thinking, Why me? I told my mother and my father about my dream. They told me that I needed to go and talk with Reverend Moore.

I called Reverend Moore. He set up an appointment with me at the church on a Saturday evening. We met in the trustee room, off the lower auditorium in the church at Nineteenth and I Streets NW. He sat behind the desk, and I sat across from him. I felt so confident that he was going to give me the answers to my questions about what

God was telling me. I took a deep breath and told him that I felt that God was calling me into the ministry. I shared with him what had happened after his sermon in New York. Then I just listened.

"Walter, you need to be very sure. The ministry is a very lonely life. It is not a profession you choose the way you choose to become a police officer or a bus driver or a mail carrier. This is a calling from God. You will find that people go into it for all the wrong reasons. Some people will do it because they want to impress people. Some have done it because they have been to prison, and they think the ministry will validate them. Others will do it because they think that there is money to be made—some ministers drive Cadillacs or Lincolns. Those are all the wrong reasons. Sometimes the longest, loneliest walk you will take is from the pulpit chair to the sacred desk to preach the word." (It is amazing how I can still remember his words just like it was yesterday, even though it was forty-eight years ago.) He then said something that made me a little more relieved. God never calls anyone who is not already busy doing something for Him in a place where He can speak to that person's heart. Reverend Moore told me that he wanted me to start working with the Children's Church, assisting the minister who was in charge of it.

I told him about the dream that I had been having for the previous three months. His face suddenly changed. He listened even more intently to me. He leaned forward, folding his hands together as if he was praying. When I finished telling him of the dream, there was a long pause as he looked intently at me. He then said, "That is most interesting." He took a sheet of paper from the desk, wrote on it, and handed it to me. On the paper, he'd written I Samuel 3.

I had never read that chapter before. He told me that what I had shared with him sounded very much like Samuel's call to be a prophet. When I got home, I went straight to my bedroom and read the chapter.

Samuel, I would later learn, was young when he was called as a prophet. He was probably about five years old, and the message God gave him was a confirmation of the message He had given to Eli concerning his house and the behavior of his wicked and disobedient sons. Three times, God called Samuel before Eli told him to answer, "Speak, Lord, for Thy servant heareth" in 1 Samuel 3:10.

After reading, I prayed, "Lord, I hear You and I will answer Your call." A peace came over me that night. There was so much that I still had to learn and so much growing I still had to do. However, I was willing to go because the Lord had called. I would be obedient, and I would answer.

I would encourage anyone who feels that God has called him or her into ministry to get training and mentoring from a caring pastor. Follow his or her lead. Don't be a maverick and think you have all the answers. Be teachable! There is nothing worse for a pastor than to have someone in his ministry who is supposed to be working with him but is unteachable. If you disagree with your pastor's teachings, you have only two options. You may choose to follow his teachings, or you may choose to go to some other church that has the teachings that you subscribe to. To challenge the shepherd of that flock is an act of sin and brings disunity to the body of Christ. You will have to answer to God for that.

You must have respect for and trust in the pastor who is mentoring and training you. I respected—and still respect—Reverend Moore for the mentoring, training, and wisdom he imparted to me. He was the son of a pastor. He had two generations of experience to pass on to me. For someone who valued the wisdom of elders, this was a gold mine. Even before my call to ministry, I had watched him from my spot in the balcony, where I could look down and see his sermon notes in that spiral notebook. It looked as though he wrote out every word of his sermons (manuscript style, I would learn later). I studied how he did the call to worship, led the responsive readings, blessed infants, pray the altar prayer, extended the invitation to Christian discipleship, and did the benediction. I watched him closely at baptisms. You name it; I observed it closely. He even shared with me the types of ministers to watch out for. He said some people go into ministry for all the wrong reasons and make a mess that the rest of us have to clean up. I was determined not to be like that. I have seen many ministers who are, however, and I've heard horror stories about many more. I was determined not to be like some of the bad situations I saw.

Sometimes people will try to "swell your head" with nonsense. I remember a situation that was most tragic. A young licensed preacher was working under a pastor, who had been at a particular church for a number of years. This pastor had baptized this young man and taken him under his wing like a son when his father passed away. The pastor had grown up in the South and had only completed tenth grade. He had taught himself to read and write. He had managed to do quite well. He read constantly and was full of wisdom that he passed on to this young man.

The young man had majored in church history, with a minor in speech, at a Christian college. An elderly member of the congregation told the young man, "You know, your preaching is so much better than the pastor's. Your grammar is better. If you were the pastor here, we would really grow leaps and bounds under you. I bet other folks feel the same way. In fact, I know some who do feel that way."

This woman had just committed several sinful acts. First, she had spoken against the man of God (gossip). Second, she had planted a seed of conceit in this young man that brought contention into that church. Third, her actions eventually caused severely broken relationships that never healed.

While making visitations that the pastor had asked him to make, this young man started subtly telling the members what he would do if he were pastor. It started a stir in the congregation. This young man thought he had the backing of the majority of the congregation to take over as pastor. A few of the members said that once that happened, they would call for an ordination council to ordain him immediately and install him as the pastor.

There was a church meeting a month later. The issue came to the floor of the meeting. The young man's mother stood up and said that if the congregation followed her son in this disgraceful act of attempting to unseat the pastor who had baptized him, nurtured him, trusted him, and treated him like a son, she would withdraw her membership immediately—even though her great-grandfather had been one of the founding members. She asked the chair of the deacon board to call for a vote to retain the pastor or relieve him of his duties. Only two people voted to relieve the pastor of his duties—the woman who'd whispered to the young preacher the poisonous words and the young preacher.

The young man's mother, with tears in her eyes, then made a motion that the church resend her son's license to preach the gospel based on his disrespect for his pastor and the leadership of that church. The vote was unanimous. The young man left the church in disgrace. To my knowledge, he made no further attempt to enter into ministry. The shame and humiliation he must have felt could have been avoided if he had a heart for Christ and had learned humility rather than being concerned about position and title. If one feels the need to speak against the pastor who is training and mentoring him or her, that person needs to find a new mentor.

You must have a servant's heart. The cold, the callous, the heartless, the ruthless, and the deceitful belong in other professions in the corporate world, not in the gospel of Jesus Christ. Anyone who desires to tend a flock of God's sheep must learn to love His sheep the way He loves them.

I learned that there is no "fast track" to the top, and there shouldn't be. That breeds arrogance and pride in a preacher—not humility and compassion. It is a slow, deliberate process. If you are serious about ministry, you will not rush or be in a hurry just because you want to stand up in front of people and preach. If you just want an audience, there are many other things you can do. Ministry is not about you, it is about serving God and His people with compassion and humility. It takes time to grow, process what you are learning as you grow, reflect on what you are learning, and apply what you are learning to your life in a way that it will stay with you. In that way, you will later be able to recall what you have learned to help others grow.

People with bully spirits should not go into ministry. Ministry by intimidation is not ministry. It is a sinful form of bondage. If it is all about your ego, don't go. A church's growth and the growth of the people can and will be hindered by intimidation, strong-arm tactics, and verbally abusive pastors, leaders, and officers. Those things destroy the harmony of a church, and it will take a long time for it to heal.

People who view ministry as "just a job or a profession" like working at a bank, in some corporate office, or at a law firm should not go into ministry. Ministry is a calling and a passion. You have to care about the people you serve. You have to have a love for them even when they are unloving to you. That is not always an easy task. Some, you will find, are hard to love. Some, you will have to love at a distance just to protect yourself and your family from the hurt they attempt to inflict.

Many people, if not most, cannot accept the pastor as being human. Other people can have flaws or make mistakes, but they seem to expect the pastor or minister to be "God junior." That is not possible. The truth is, a minister is human like everyone else, but God has chosen him or her to perform a ministry that is different from those of the congregation. God has the same standard for all of His followers. When a pastor or minister falls, people are threatened, in many cases, because it forces them to look at their own flaws and frailties. Instead of butchering the person, why not pray for and seek to restore that person to a fellowship relationship with God and the people of God? That is what He does for each of us when we fall daily.

Reverend Moore took his time with me and did not set me up to preach my initial sermon until I was in my second year of college. I was blessed that he gave me opportunities to preach, as did Reverend Clark in Youngstown, Ohio; Rev. Norman Smith in Rectortown, Virginia; and Rev. Benjamin Simmons in Philadelphia. They didn't have to do it. They just did, and for that, I am thankful.

A pastor has charge of the pulpit in his or her church and does not have to invite anyone into it to preach. He or she makes those choices. I never asked anyone to let me preach or assumed that he would. That would have been arrogance on my part. One thing that is not becoming is a "pushy preacher." That is a turnoff for most people.

It was difficult enough to know deep down in my spirit at age fourteen that God had called me to preach and not declare it to my parents or my pastor until I turned sixteen. Add to that the normal challenges that go with being a sixteen-year-old male—figuring out who I was and what my purpose in the world was, coupled with wanting to serve and please God while still having a lot of growing to do. Along with that, I was dealing with an undiagnosed learning disability that was interpreted as "laziness" in school. It forced me to find strategies to cope with being a slow reader. I learned how to use a highlighter to find the important points in what I was reading. The color helped make the words stand out on the page. I found it easy to read human-interest stories and anything to do with trains, streetcars, or subways. It was also easy to read the Bible. I started to develop a passion for reading about people who overcame awful life situations—bondage by horrific monster-type personalities in their lives—and then went on to do great and wonderful things. So, I continued growing from the age at which God called me to the time I preached my initial sermon at twenty. Then, when I was twenty-three, God took me deeper.

Reverend Moore also taught me that unless I was going into some special field of mission where there would be no ordained clergyperson, or there was a need for it at the church, or I was being called to pastor a church, there was no need for me to be ordained. He did not call for the church to convene an ordination council until I was called as pastor of the Mount Carmel Baptist Church in Blainesville, Virginia, in June 1973. Mount Carmel Baptist Church sent a letter to Nineteenth Street Baptist Church requesting that the church convene an ordination council.

He assigned Rev. Aubrey Lewis, a son of the church who was ordained the year I was licensed to preach, and Rev. James Godfrey, who had been assistant to the pastor, to coach me for ordination. I was given the mainstay book in the African American Baptist Church to study, *Hiscox's Standard Manual for Baptist Churches*, by Edward T. Hiscox. I was told what types of questions would be covered in the examination. That is when the awesomeness of this calling I had answered began to dawn on me. I would have to be able to share with conviction my salvation experience and my call to the ministry of the gospel of Jesus Christ. I would have to answer questions on Baptist Church doctrine and be willing to show evidence by my conviction that I believed the Bible was the infallible word of God and a "perfect treasure of heavenly instruction." I would have to answer many questions to give evidence of my knowledge and understanding of Baptist Church doctrine, polity, policy, and procedures. I was now beginning to understand why Rev. Dr. Jerry Moore took his time and did not rush to get me ordained. There was so much he wanted me to know about the church doctrine and beliefs. There was so much he wanted to pass on to me, and he wanted to be certain that I would to take it to heart and hold it dear—not just about church doctrine but also about a relationship with Christ.

During the process of studying for ordination, I had a profound experience. It occurred during my last year of college, on February 19, 1973. I had observed a friend at school who was upset about something. She went to the cafeteria, sat down at a table, opened her Bible, and said she needed to "hear from the Lord." I had never heard anyone talk about the Lord in quite that way. I watched her from a distance because what she said fascinated me. She was reading in the Gospel of John. Something she read must have spoken to her spirit because her face began to glow. She took her highlighter and highlighted the verses. Then she folded her hands and prayed, sitting at that table in the cafeteria, while tears of obvious joy flowed down her face. I had never seen anyone in my age bracket respond like that or speak in such a personal way of a relationship with the Lord. It was so intimate. That was what Uncle Louis, Aunt Cinnie, my grandmothers, and Granddaddy Jackson had that I thought was just for older people. I wanted to know the Lord at that level. If she could have it at our age, I wanted it too! I had to have it! I was determined I was going to get before God somehow and meet Him in the same way she met Him.

That night, I decided to read the Gospel of John. Was there something there I had missed? Was there something about "going to church" I had not been seeing or hearing? How was it she seemed to be "best friends" with the Lord, while I seemed to be missing that? I had to find the answer.

I must have read for about an hour when I decided to say my prayers and go to sleep. I got down on my knees to pray the Lord's Prayer as I always did, but this time the words that came out of my mouth were different. "Lord, I believe that You have saved me. If You have, I need to know for sure right now. I believe that You have filled me with Your spirit; I need to know right now. Thank You, Lord, amen."

I started to get up off my knees, but I could not move. It was as though I were frozen. I began to confess my sins to Him—everything I could think of that I had ever done wrong. The more I did, the more refreshed and lighter I felt. When I finally got up, I got into bed and began to read John again. This time, it was as if the words were jumping off the page at me. I cried as I read about the crucifixion and the burial of Jesus. I smiled when I read about the resurrection and realized that someday, Jesus is coming back for me.

Then I was able to go to sleep.

At school the next day, everyone one was staring at me. God has a way of confirming what He has done. My classmates kept saying, "You look different. Something has changed. You are glowing." Several classmates pulled me into the choir room and asked me what had happened. With tears in my eyes, I explained what had happened the night before. There was such a rejoicing as I shared it with them. I knew then just how real Jesus is. I met Him that night in my bedroom in a very real way.

I continued to prepare for my ordination with a new conviction as to why God had been speaking to me all those years. He had been drawing me, wooing me, and leading me to a place where He could be intimate with me. How could anyone preach with conviction, passion, and power without having a *true* love relationship with Christ? How can any man or woman just decide to go into ministry the way you choose a secular job? Yet people do it. Knowing "church rhetoric and mannerisms" does not give you a ticket into heaven. There must be an ongoing, intimate relationship with Christ that grows daily, just as the relationships between husbands and wives or parents and children grow from the time of the marriage or the birth of the child to death. That is how a relationship with Christ must grow.

So, I continued to study and prepare with a new understanding, love, and passion for the one who had been calling to me for all those years. However, now I struggled with a question in the final months of preparation for my ordination. Should I listen to some of my friends, who were not Baptist, who said, "Now that you are *truly* saved, you need to come out from among them and be separate from them"?

You should be with us, they said.

I continued to pray and study. I knew God had called me to preach. Was He also calling me to leave the Baptist church? As I studied my Bible and the church doctrine, I realized that it was a faith journey of which I had to be convinced in my own mind. The confirmation came when one of my close friends, a member of a Pentecostal denomination, told me, "I would love to have you in fellowship with me at my church. However, if everyone who really understood the true meaning of salvation left the churches where they were and joined another that focused more on the relationship with Christ, how would others get to hear and know the good news of Jesus?

"You stay where you are," he said. "God needs you there! You have many to reach there! You will make a difference right there in the Baptist church. That is where God has called you to work."

How prophetic were his words! Forty-one years later, even with many battle scars and pains, I am glad I listened to the words he gave me. I thank God that his wife, my friend and classmate, Rev. Dr. Betty Lancaster Short, went into the college cafeteria on that February day just to "hear from God." I thank God that the late Bishop Stephen N. Short gave me that prophetic advice that caused me to stay where God wanted me to be and attempt to have an impact on the lives of others by showing them just how real Christ desires to be in our lives.

And They Laid Their Hands on Me—the Ordination, July 7, 1973
Some moments in your life stand out and remain as fresh as if they happened five minutes ago. For me, July 7, 1973, the day of my ordination to the gospel ministry, was one of them.

I must share that the one sad note to my ordination was that on a Saturday night in March 1973, Grandma Graham went home to be with the Lord while she slept. I was devastated, but I knew that I would see her again because I now knew the same Jesus that she knew and was ready to see when He came for her. My sadness was that she was not able to be present for my ordination as she had been when I preached my initial sermon. However, Granddaddy Jackson and Grandma Jackson sat there proudly alongside my mom and my dad. Granddaddy was so intense. I found out later from Daddy that Granddaddy had wanted to go into ministry, but his father discouraged him. My great-grandfather Jackson was Catholic, and Nana was Baptist. During the 1890s and early 1900s, a kind of rivalry existed. My great-grandfather told my grandfather that if he ever saw him in a Protestant pulpit, he would beat him out of it. That is what I was told. Until the day he died, my granddaddy took a keen interest in my ministry. I believe that he vicariously lived out his desire to be in ministry through me.

Among those who came to my ordination were friends from college, my godmother, friends I attended Bible studies with, coworkers from my summer job in the National Park Service, church members, neighbors, family members, and, of course, the band of ministers who formed the ordination council. It was a long process, and it was an open examination—the public was invited to sit in. Some associations have gone to closed sessions and or written examinations.

To protect the integrity of the process, I will not go into specific questions asked at an ordination. But categories covered are the candidate's salvation experience; call to the gospel ministry; and basic knowledge of the Bible, God, man, and the doctrines and ordinances of the Baptist faith.

One person is designated to ask the questions in each category, and then some of the ministers on the council ask follow-up questions if the candidate didn't answer to their satisfaction. This lasts for several hours as the candidate sits or stands in the front of the church while he or she is grilled. When the questions are over, they send the candidate out while they deliberate and decide whether to ordain him or her. If the vote is yes, the candidate is called back in, told the news, and they proceed with the ordination worship service. There is a scripture, a hymn, and a sermon, and then all of those ministers have the candidate kneel down, and they lay their hands on his or her head, and one of them prays an ordination prayer. After helping the candidate to his feet, shaking his hand, and embracing him as a sign of welcome into the clergy, one of the ministers on the council presents the new minister with a Bible and gives him a solemn charge to "Preach the word: be instant in season and out of season; (2Timothy 4:2a).

Little did I know the impact of those words then as I do now, four decades later. (We'll talk about that in another chapter.)

While the council deliberated whether to ordain me, I was sent to the pastor's study to await the decision. I was mentally exhausted but strangely calm. I had fasted the day before and that morning. I was at peace. My dad came back to check on me. I had never seen my dad so excited. He always seemed so calm. He seemed to beam with pride. If nothing else, I felt affirmed by his support and his love as I had never felt before. Nothing else in the world mattered at that moment. He said Granddaddy and Grandma were so proud of how well I answered the questions of the council. He said my mother still had tears flowing down her face. I told him that I only wished that Grandma Graham could have been there. He said something that made me remember those words she would say to me when I would get sleepy while doing homework. He told me he believed that God had allowed her to see it all from heaven and that she was happy too. I felt that I heard her say, "Keep at it, son!" It was at that moment that Reverend Moore came to the study and told my dad to bring me back to the sanctuary.

As I stood on the same spot where I had been questioned nonstop for almost two hours and forty minutes, the moderator of the ordination council announced to me that it was a unanimous decision to set me aside for the gospel ministry from that day forward. I had answered their questions well and had proven myself to be called to serve our Lord in that capacity. They voted to proceed immediately with the ordination worship.

The service moved forward as I outlined. After the late Dr. Henry C. Gregory preached the ordination sermon from Hebrews 12:1–3 (running the race), I was called up to the pulpit in front of the "great croud of witnesses" and asked to kneel down. There, behind the sacred desk where I had preached my initial sermon and above the baptismal pool where, seventeen years earlier to the day, I had been baptized; there with the hands of all of those ministers who had just questioned me on my head; I humbly knelt down before God, my friends, my family, and the ministers. They laid hands on me and prayed with such power and intensity for God to use me under His Holy Ghost power that I shook like someone shivering in severely cold weather. Tears flowed down my face. I could hear the minister praying and people answering with shouts of "amen" and "thank you, Jesus!" or with sniffles and cries. I felt as though I was shrinking within myself, becoming smaller and smaller as a warm presence came into me. The voice I heard in my spirit said, "Walter, I am Jesus. I will be with you always. Keep at it!"

At that same moment, the preacher who was praying shouted, "Jesus, use him, Lord, for your glory!" My tears began to fall to the floor. The noise from the congregation was such that I could not tell which congregants were Baptists and which were my Methodist friends or my Pentecostal friends. It was just some worship noise in that church that Saturday afternoon. Never had I felt such intense power and energy going through me. As I write this recount of that long-ago day, it is as fresh in my spirit as if it were five minutes ago. Every ordination is different. I am sure that every minister who is called of God can identify in some way with this experience. I have participated in many ordinations since then and have the responsibility of training candidates for ordination in my association. I always want the candidates to know the material, know why they are going into ministry, and to know that they are saved. The last one is the most important. If the person is not saved, the rest can't happen.

It is one thing to know the material for ordination—church structure, church polity, procedures, organization, and rituals. These things mean nothing if you have no relationship with Christ, Who is the head of the church. You cannot teach someone to have a calling. A calling is something that only God can give to whom He chooses. The scripture tells us to make sure of our calling.

Set Aside to Nurture and Care for the People of God

> A charge to keep I have
> A God to glorify,
> A never-dying soul to save,
> And fit it for the sky.

These are the words from a hymn called "A Charge to Keep," written by Charles Wesley in 1762 and now in the public domain. They are from the first verse of the song. Ironically, I had never heard that song until I was ordained and the words were quoted. It would be ten years later that I would hear it sung when I was installed as pastor of the Wainwright Baptist Church. However, those words would ring in my ears for years to come from the day of my ordination. They would remind me that I was not hired as a preacher the way someone is hired to work in a store or restaurant, or as a civil servant. I was set aside by the Holy Spirit, by the laying on of hands, to nurture and care for the people of God. I was set aside to be one of those with the earthly responsibility to look after the "sheep of God's pasture" (Psalms 95:7 and 100:3). That is a sacred trust! What an awesome responsibility! I would think of this many times over the years, and I would come compare that charge to the oath that the president of the United States takes to defend the United States against foes foreign and domestic.

Sometimes pastors must nurture, care for, and protect the people of God from people within the church. It really distresses me when I see and hear of people who do things to hurt God's children. I can understand how Jesus could take a string of gourds, make a whip, and drive money changers from His Father's house. He was angry! How dare people think that preachers shouldn't get angry! The scripture says, "Be angry and sin not." When I see people attempt to do things to hurt God's people, all my wrong buttons are pushed! Some of the things I have seen and heard are horror stories that would curl straight hair and straighten curled hair. Yes, these things go on in the church. Not everybody in the church is saved, nor does everyone have a desire to be. This is nothing new. This was a fact that Jesus dealt with when He talked about the legalists of His time, the scribes, Sadducees, and the Pharisees. Jesus said to beware of their poison.

The nurturing and caring for God's people is based on love. The love is first a love you must have for God. Then, because you love God, you must love His people enough to care for them the way He cares for you. A pastor must have the gift of compassion. You can't be "fake and fabulous," as a friend of mind once put it. People can see through a phony. You must be filled with a genuine Spirit-filled concern for God's people. The people will know when you genuinely love them and are caring for them. Even if you don't have all of the answers in every situation, they will, in most cases, work with you and affirm you as their pastor if they see that you are sincere in your efforts to advocate for them, if they see that you serve them with all your heart, and if they see that you make every attempt to do what is right in the sight of God on their behalf and pray for them constantly. If you preach Jesus to them with power, sincerity, and truth, God will affirm you in your work and bless what you put your hands to do.

> To serve the present age,
> My calling to fulfill:
> Oh, may it all my pow'rs engage
> To do my master's will!
> (The second verse of "A Charge to Keep I Have")

It is amazing how the words of this hymn written so long ago still ring true today. They were even put to common meter in the African American Baptist churches in the South. Sung without music or instruments, these common-meter songs would be so moving they would make the fine hairs on the back your neck stand at attention!

A pastor must be as protective of the church and people that God has entrusted to him as a lion protecting its cubs—gentle with the cubs but a terror to anything that would harm them. This kind of love does not happen overnight. It is a love that grows over time, like a marriage. Just as Secret Service agents are trained to protect the president at all cost, even if it means personal injury or the loss of their lives, a pastor often gets abuse, verbal attacks, hate mail, and sometimes even worse to stand for God and to protect the flock of God. I was told that the longest walk I would take as a pastor would be from the pulpit chair to the sacred desk to deliver the word of God. Though the distance had not changed—only a few short steps—the walk has gotten longer and longer with each challenge, with each blessing, each pain, each sorrow, each joy, each new experience, each new monster, each monster defeated, and each reflection on what God has done. You take a long walk every time you get up to deliver the word of God to His people. All of those things go through your mind. Yet, every time I get up and take that long walk that only has a few steps, I hear God using my grandma Graham's words to encourage me. "Keep at it!"

Arm me with jealous care,
As in Thy sight to live;
And O Thy servant, Lord, prepare
And strict account to give!
(The third verse of "A Charge to Keep I Have")

Your Care Is Not Always Welcome

There are times that a pastor will find that some in the flock reject his pastoral care. It is hard not to take that personally. Sometimes, in the case of younger pastors, older members feel that you don't know enough—they have children or grandchildren older than you are. Sometimes they are angry about decisions you have made, or they didn't vote for you to be the pastor. The reasons are too numerous to mention. You still have to love them and pastor them regardless of how they treat you or talk about you, and yes, even if they hate you. (I know; that's a hard and bitter pill to swallow.) There are times when some of the members will work hard to make sure you are the very last person to know of their illnesses, hospital stays, family crises, or economic tragedies. There are times when you ask, "Why didn't you let me know?" You will hear something like, "Well, I figured somebody would tell you" or "I thought you knew!" (I call that the "osmosis syndrome." Somehow, they thought that the news would just sink in to you.) It breaks your heart when the people that you vowed to watch, protect, nurture, teach, and attempt to prepare for heaven won't trust you to help them through their difficult times. Some people learn to trust you; others never grow to that place. You just have to pray for them that they will not influence the rest of the congregation with the spirit of negativity (another monster). You just have to do the best you can with them. Bathe them in prayer daily. Sometimes, God has to take away a heart or two of stone and give a heart of flesh to those who are reluctant to have a caring pastor. In cases like that, you just have to pray and turn them over to God. Some of them, God will give over to a reprobate mind. But you must remember that how He handles them is not *your* business. It is His. You must however, remain faithful and true to God and to your call to preach the word. You must be instant in season and out of season.

> Help me to watch and pray,
> And on Thyself rely,
> Assured, if I my trust betray,
> I shall forever die.
> (The fourth verse of "A Charge to Keep I Have")

5

THE PASTORATE HAS ITS CHALLENGES

Even though the pastorate is a most rewarding experience, it can also produce some battle scars and open wounds that, in many cases, don't heal easily. At the time of this writing, I have had the privilege of being an ordained clergyman for forty-one years, between pastoral assignments, and associate and assistant to the pastor assignments, and youth pastor assignments. In these forty-one years at several independent churches, one thing I have learned is that not everyone who sits in the pew on Sunday morning is always your friend. There are several types of people you will run into at every church unless Jesus has truly entered the hearts of the people. These types are very obvious in small churches in small communities, where everyone either is related in some way or has had family ties to a particular church for generations. Here are the people types you will run into.

The control person feels the church would not be where it is if it were not for him, his money, and his connections or influence. Nobody knows how to run it better than he does. This person will go all out to make sure things are done his way, even if it means destroying others in the process.

I have found there are four kinds of people in the church when it comes to the pastor. There are pastor-blind pastor supporters, pastor supporters, pastor haters, and the let's-kill-him-if-we-can type, who generally extend that animosity to anybody who wants to follow the pastor's leadership.

I will not be discussing any specific persons or situations that have happened in my church out of respect and love for the members. As I mentioned earlier, as for the rest of my life situations I will not dignify any specific monsters or demons by naming them. We often pay too much attention to monsters and their antics. That validates them, which should not happen. I *can* share some cases that I know of, some horror stories that have happened to other pastors, or incidents that people have told me of, but I will not mention the names of the churches, towns, states, denominations, or conventions where any of these situations took place. Some of these stories may sound similar to situations you know of. That is merely a coincidence. What I have found is that similar things take place in every church setting where people are not focused on the Lord but on the flesh and the things of the world and the ways of the world.

I believe that if Jesus were to walk into many of our churches today, He would once again make a whip of gourds and beat some people— those with bad attitudes or controlling spirits, gossips, discouragers, babe-in-Christ killers (discouragers of new Christians), the criticizers of hardworking saints, and the pastor destroyers. He would probably take the whip to some pastors, too, I am sorry to say. I have seen situations in many churches where certain people or groups feel the need to disrespect the pastor of the church, push their personal agendas, and discount anything scriptural. These are the same types of people that Jesus cautioned against. They are modern-day Pharisees and Sadducees.

Smiles and Knives

As a pastor, you will find that there are those who love you and those who hate you. There will also be those who love to hate you and delight in doing so. The ones who love you will love you unconditionally and support you. They may disagree with you at times, but they still love and respect you as pastor.

You will find at times that some will deliberately say things within earshot of your wife and children just to be hurtful and vindictive, while pretending they have never said a word or done an unkind deed. Hate mail and anonymous letters may be written and smear campaigns carried out against you, and yet each Lord's day, you must stand before the people that God has entrusted into your care and preach Christ and Him crucified with love and true conviction, as though they have never done you any harm. Remember whose footsteps we are walking in. We are following Christ's example of service. They are not going to treat you any better than they treated Jesus! The only thing different is that He had to die! They killed Him because of His love for us. Surely, I can live because of my love for Him in spite of all the monsters that have come up against me. I am sure each of you has faced some monsters too.

I am sure people in every profession confront monsters. You just have to be true to yourself and to God, and you will heap hot coals upon them. The best thing you can do for your enemies is to hold your head up, treat them cordially, and don't stoop to their level of despicable deeds and tactics. Kindness will eventually kill hatred or cause it to leave you alone for a season. You can never let the monsters in your life control your purpose and your destiny. If you do, you are validating their control over you. You must rise above them.

There will be smiles in ministry, just as there are knives. I tend to want to see the whole world through rose-colored glasses. Growing up my mother had rose bushes in our back yard. I hated having to prune them and gather up the thorny branches for the trash. I love the smell of roses; I just hate dealing with the thorns! I think someone developed roses that have no thorns. I will have to check that out. Maybe if they have, I plant some in my outdoor garden railroad when I rebuild it to run my indoor/outdoor trains in the flower garden, in memory of my mother and the lessons I learned from dealing with thorns.

It is the smiles in ministry that keep you doing ministry, even when you feel like throwing in the towel because of control issues, power struggles, or territorial battles over who should do what or who seems to be doing all the work in the ministry and church. Maybe that person does the work because no one else will step forward to say, "How can I help?" That happens so many times in so many churches. Yet each week, committed and loving pastors swallow hurt and pain to preach Jesus. Then they return home to continue bandaging their wounds.

I asked a friend who had been a pastor for over forty years, "Why did you stay with those people after the way they treated you and your family? They put outright lies out on you. Some of them sent anonymous letters and other hate mail, and spoke nastily to your children to get at you. They grinned in your face and talked about you like a dog behind your back. Some even disrupted worship, breathing hatred because you listened to what God was saying to you and not to what they had on their agenda! That is just wrong! Look what it did to your health! Why did you stay?"

He answered, "Yes, they did." Then he asked me a question. "What did the people do to Jesus? Why did He stay on the cross for them? That is why I stayed in His church—for Him, not for the people but for Him and because of Him." Those were words I shall never forget. They left a deep impression on me. He said, "If and when it is time to leave, you will know because He will tell you. He will have someplace else for you to go." Again, my grandma Graham would say, "Keep at it!"

I often think of Grandma Graham's advice as she watched me struggling with homework, frustrated, tired, and sleepy. Yet she sat with me and encouraged me with that sentence, "Keep at it!" Even now as I enter my home after a challenging day as a pastor or a school employee, I can see her sitting on the sofa, which now resides in my living room. Just as when I was a school transportation supervisor, or a substitute teacher, or a Metrobus driver, or a college student, she says, "Keep at it!" She has said that quite often in the last few years.

Every time I preach and the anointing falls and the presence of God surrounds me to let me know He is pleased, I hear her voice saying, "Keep at it!" There is a driving force inside me that compels me to want to be more effective in reaching God's people with His word and finding better ways to minister to the unsaved.

I wonder sometimes why Jesus didn't just come out and say, "Your enemies you have with you always" along with saying, "The poor you have with you always." At least in most cases, the poor appreciate what you do. They don't attempt to tear you down or destroy what you stand for. However, love them all, we must! That is a mandate from God. I don't want you to think that I am saying that all preachers and pastors are above being in the category of "enemies." Even we in ministry can and do cross the line into the sin of mistreating the membership and fellow clergy with our words or deeds. God will hold us accountable also! Again, it is better that a millstone be tied about your neck and you be cast into the sea than to harm one of the children of God. That is what His word says. Yet people do it weekly and then sing hymns, testify, and shout behind their actions. I have three words for that behavior: carnal, carnal, and carnal! A long time ago, a blind woman told me, "Watch the ones who sing loud and shout high. They just might be the ones to hit you in the lowest part of your belly." Sometimes those words have rung true.

I heard a story at a meeting recently that sent a chill down my spine because I had heard of similar scenarios before. A pastor was elected, and the "honeymoon" period started. The previous pastor had died, and this new pastor had just been installed. He was met by the trustees, who said, "Pastor, now that you are here, we should redo your office with new furniture." The existing furniture was not very old at all and in excellent condition.

They began to exert pressure to influence pastoral decisions. When other ministries within the church began to share their concerns and desires with the pastor, the trustees did not want him to listen to what these members had to say.

The trustees had taken the stand that no pastoral decision could be made without their approval. They expected the pastor to clear every decision with them—when he would accept outside preaching engagements, who he would invite to preach at the church, and what he would put on the agenda for meetings of the membership. When the trustees saw that the pastor was going to stand his ground and not bow to these ungodly demands, they rose up against him and created a stir in the church. Though he was encouraged by many in the congregation to fight them, he chose to leave instead of splitting the church. He later went on to do quite well at another church in another state. The first church eventually got rid of a few ungodly trustees before calling a new pastor.

I was told of a similar situation in another area of the country. One person who was angry because he was no longer in control of the finances set out to destroy the finance administrator. The smear campaign wreaked havoc in the entire community. It damaged the church's witness and hurt innocent members, while the demonic influences saw no wrong in what they did. Those without conscience usually don't see the damage they do, nor do they care.

Worship services were disrupted, and one day, the congregation stood with the pastor and said, "You will not hurt our church or another child of the King!" The bad actors were removed from their respective ministries immediately. This ring of former leaders left the church in embarrassment, humiliation, and shame. The church went through a very long healing process. The finance administrator still holds his head up high and is loved and respected as a man of integrity as he continues to do his job with great Christian humility.

These stories are just two of many I've heard. The first one took place in a West Coast church, and the second, in a midwestern church. I could share several other stories that are so similar they would make you scream. I have heard stories like these from churches in other denominations. Yet in each case, the pastor and the members that bore the brunt of ungodly, sinful knives, kept at the work of the Lord because of their love for God. Though the pain and the scars inflicted had damaging effects on each of the congregations, they "kept at it" in spite of the odds. God had His way of taking care of each situation. In each case, He took care of it very well.

Not all "church people" act that way or are mean, calculating, and vindictive. Many take the word of God and their relationship with Him and His people seriously.

Many of us who have been hurt in various situations would tell you that the relationship we have with Christ is worth more than whatever we have gone through at the hands of others. Though there are times when the pain is so great that it is almost unbearable, something drives you to hold onto "God's Unchanging Hand" (an old hymn in the Baptist Church) and you keep at it.

In every situation, God always gives peace in the storms, calm in the valleys of the shadow of death, and grace through all floods of evil brought by Satan. God *never* leaves His children who are thrown under the streetcar! He loves us too much. When you feel like giving up, God does something to give you a personal revival. Sometimes those personal revivals come in the middle of your worst moments. They often happen when someone who is smiling has his foot on your neck. Those are the best revivals!

I cannot begin to tell you how wonderful it is when God refreshes you after a dry spell in your ministry. The dry spells are the challenges, obstacles, the crises, and the times when difficult people become stumbling blocks to ministry and to the work of the Lord. They happen in every church, ministry, and every pastor's administration. Some situations are worse than others are. Some are mere walks through brown dry grass, while other dry spells turn into full-blown wilderness experiences, complete with cynical complainers and prophets of doom.

I was just sharing with a pastor whom I recently met that one of the most rewarding things I have ever done in my life is to pastor a church, and one of the most painful things I have ever done in my life is to pastor a church. It is a *calling*, not a job, as I have said previously.

Years ago, a friend told me about a deacon who had controlled a church for about sixty years. He had managed to take charge of the Deacon Board when his father died. He had the only key to the building, and he guarded it closely. The church did what he wanted, or the doors were not opened on Sunday morning. The trustees were afraid to challenge him because several of them rented homes from him and did not want to be sitting on the curb. He delighted in calling the pastor a "young boy who didn't know anything." The church had a business meeting on a Saturday evening and was discussing who to hire to do some work on the church. The deacon wanted his nephew to do the work, and the congregation wanted an outside contractor. The church voted for the outside contractor. The deacon yelled and screamed, telling the members that the vote was going to cost them dearly. The next day, it did. When Sunday dawned in the Pennsylvania hills, the temperature was twelve degrees. The members stood outside in the cold, waiting to see if the deacon would come down and unlock the doors.

After a while, they had an emergency meeting just to change the vote to let the deacon's nephew have the contract to do the work on the church. They sent one of the members to tell the deacon that the vote had been changed. The man arrogantly came down to the church, unlocked the door, and said, "Now, you are ready to have church!" He turned to the young pastor and said, "Boy, I run things here, and don't you forget it!" The young pastor was speechless. However, he prayed, and on Monday, he called a locksmith. The locks on all the doors were changed, and the trustees were given keys. When they saw what their young pastor had done, two of the trustees had enough nerve to stand up to the deacon and his bullying spirit. They moved their families out of the deacon's houses and broke that stronghold. One was able to buy his own home right away. That was also the last contract that the deacon's nephew ever got from the church. After that, every contract was awarded by sealed bid. The elderly deacon continued to be a "thorn in the flesh" of everyone, spreading rumors, gossip, and outright lies throughout the small community about those who had stood up to him and opposed him. He referred to the pastor as that crazy #$%#@ boy! (You can imagine what #$%#@ stands for.) One day about a year after the incident, he had a severe stroke on his right side. He lost his ability to speak and was sent to a nursing home, where he spent three years until his passing.

There are hundreds of similar situations around the country, in which controlling people or groups have bullied pastors and churches for their own purposes and agendas. They may think they are acting in the will of God, but in fact, Satan and all the forces of hell are driving them. These things grieve the Lord and His church. The good news is that the Lord will not let these things slide under the spiritual rug. He will not let His church fail.

I believe every true "shepherd-hearted pastor" deals with people and situations like these in his or her ministry. The names may change, the situations may change, the backgrounds of the troubled and hurting troublemakers may be different, but there is a similar footprint and pattern to each. They lie in wait in every church, big or small, in every state, city, and town, in every hamlet and village or township. Those are the knives that come at you sharpened and ready for the kill. They try to rob you of your sleep and take your focus off sermon preparation and caring for the people of God.

A true pastor will love all of the people, no matter what spirit they come with. I have learned that I can't be in fellowship with some of the people I love; I have to love them from a distance. But I love them just the same.

I often get a picture of what it must have been like for Jesus to be hanging at Calvary, dying on a cross in open shame as an act of sacrifice and love for a bunch of angry people who were yelling at him, spitting on him, cursing at him, and saying, *Crucify Him!*" In the midst of all that, He could stop looking at the people and what they were doing and muster "keep at it" strength until the moment of death. He could say, "Father forgives them because they don't know what they are doing." Is that not *love*? Is that not what Christians are called to do? It is not as easy as it sounds, I know. Sometimes the very ones we are called to minister to may well be the ones crying, "Kill! Kill! Kill!" Sometimes the action you must take will not be popular, but if it is right in the sight of God, if it protects the integrity and sanctity of His church and protects His people, then act, you must. And know that the Lord is with you, even in the midst of the knives.

Even though it may not always seem like it, there is always someone smiling at you with encouragement, love, and peace. The devils only *seem* to exist in large numbers because they make loud noises. Smiles are quiet, yet soothing.

I am not a fan of baseball, basketball, or football. However, I watch the Super Bowl most of the time. It is usually a good time to fellowship with friends. In the game between the Seahawks and the Patriots, there were some amusing commercials. God used one of them to speak to me about how He stands with us and how there are people that smile with us that we don't even realize. This ad also struck a nerve because I think horses are beautiful animals, and I have three Labrador retrievers; two are brother and sister (Kobe and Queenie, ten years old and born in my home). The third one, Duke, I rescued from a friend when he found out that his girlfriend was allergic to him. This commercial was for Budweiser beer. In it, a Lab puppy wanders off, gets lost, and then attempts to find his way home. The puppy's owner and the Clydesdale horses are sad and miss the puppy. That cute little yellow Lab gets close to home and begins to bark. But a wolf is standing in the path, blocking the way, growling, and showing his teeth. Meanwhile, a horse that the dog had bonded with hears the bark. The horse kicks open the door of his stall and rallies the other Clydesdales. They run to the field and stand like an army behind the puppy. The wolf runs away, deciding that fight is not worth having. I believe those horses would have put something on that wolf that Clorox would not take off. The next thing you see is the little dog leading the herd of horses back home, where the owner cleans him up, embraces him, and loves him.

God spoke to me that night through that beer commercial, showing me how much that story is like being the pastor of the church. We go out into the hedges and the highways, among dangers seen and unseen, in storms and through fiery darts. Sometimes the journey seems uncertain, and the path is not always clear. Wolves growl and snap at you. Often they will do that while you minister the word of God. Yet there are those that are genuinely smiling at you and love you who will knock down the gates of hell and bondage to stand with you and uphold you because *you* are the one who is leading them home to Christ. The pastor's reward is that the Lord will bathe our wounds upon our arrival, wipe away our tears, erase our pain and sorrow, and embrace us with His love for the church. The people we ministered to in this life stand as the "great cloud of witnesses" of how we "kept at it" in the heat of the day and in the midst of the battle. God showed me this entire scenario during, of all things, a Bud commercial during the Super Bowl!

Encouragement and Hate Mail

Although I am not a big fan of the major national sports, I have always loved a good pep rally. I used to go to the games just so I could cheer as the cheerleaders led the cheers for the crowd. My extreme near sightedness prevented me from playing ball games. Instead, I ran track for a while. However, something magical happens at a pep rally and at a ball game when the crowd loudly, and without shame or inhibition, cheers its team toward a victory. The people in the stands are the encouragers. They will brave cold weather, snow, and rain to stand by and encourage the team. The yelling, whistling, screaming, crazy costumes, and the catchy chant of the cheerleaders and the band all help the players to keep their focus and keep at it. It often seems that the harder the crowd cheers, the harder the team plays.

I remember when I went to my first pep rally in high school, when tenth grade was the first year of high school. The assistant principal of Anacostia High School, Mr. Lombardi, who would, the next year, become principal, announced a pep rally in the gymnasium. I don't think any of us in the tenth grade were sure what to expect from a pep rally. The rest of the school seemed excited. As the tenth graders arrived in the gym, the eleventh and twelfth graders were already there, cheering. They were showing us how it was done (Anacostia style). The drum line was beating out a cadence, and the people in the stands were chanting in a rhythmic beat resembling a jazzy gospel beat. The crowd was clapping, stomping, and saying/singing:

Hey, hey, hey, hey, hey. We gotta win!
Hey, hey, hey, hey, hey. We gotta win!
Hey, hey, hey, hey, hey. We gotta win!

Now, I was not sold on the game, but I certainly was sold on pep rallies! You got goose bumps! There was an energy that is, even to this day, hard to describe. It was like an intense church revival without the churchy trappings, setting, and words. This was before the team came into the gym. It was like old-style African American, Deep South church devotions before the pastor comes into the sanctuary! For some of you younger folks who are not familiar with that, it was as if the praise team caused the congregation to rise spontaneously to its feet in praise. Twelve hundred students were acting and sounding as one voice, one unit, one school, and they were supporting one team. What an experience! What a moment! I thought, "So, this is a pep rally!" Then Mr. Lombardi walked out on the floor. He thanked the students for their good behavior as they cheered wildly. He then introduced the football coach, Mr. Colona. Mr. Colona introduced the players one by one, and the crowd went wild, stomping on the bleachers, screaming, and cheering. After Mr. Colona had called all of the names, there were high fives among the team members, drumbeats, screams, yells, and flips by cheerleaders. I had never witnessed such solidarity, such encouragement, and such a bond. The school band played the school song, "Hail to Anacostia," and we walked back to our next-period class. I will never forget that experience, and I remember it like it was this morning.

When the crowd cheered, it motivated the team to play like mad men. They were pushed to play hard on behalf of the school and their classmates. If one of them became injured, the crowd went silent until the player was back on his feet or had been helped off the field or the court. At that point, everyone would cheer wildly. That must have been so encouraging for the injured team member to know he was supported and affirmed in such a powerful way. Days after a game, even if the team had lost, there was still that affirming support from the school.

I have often thought of that pep rally as a school system employee, watching middle school cheerleaders and sports teams connect in that same way. As I was beginning to write this book, the Lord spoke to me about how the church (the body of believers in Christ) should encourage the pastor. As he or she "stands in the gap" for the congregation, the membership should be the pep rally of encouragement for the pastor. The pastor is not perfect. He is a forgiven sinner saved by grace, just as the members are, but with a calling and anointing to stand before them proclaiming the gospel of Jesus Christ and to lead them to victory over personal, family, physical, emotional, and spiritual issues in their lives. If you keep the pastor encouraged, then he or she will work that much harder to meet the needs of the congregation. Just as that sports team is motivated by the encouragement from the crowd, the pastor is motivated and encouraged by the people in his or her congregation. When you encourage the pastor, it has the same effect as encouraging a sports team to victory.

The encouragement causes the committed and sincere pastor to think of more ways, better ways, and more powerful ways to minister effectively to the people God has entrusted to him or her. Just as an athlete will play with minor injuries by wrapping joints and other injured areas for the sake of carrying the team to victory, the pastor will push on to serve the congregation in spite of the naysayers, backstabbers, gossipers, downright haters, and character assassins if there is encouragement from those in the congregation who stand with him or her in worship and praise (the pep rally). Those pastors will endure personal pain for the cause of Christ and for the sake of the members that support and love their pastor. That kind of encouragement cannot be measured in dollars and cents. It can only be assessed by what it does in your soul and in the lives of the congregation you serve. When you know and feel that you are valued and appreciated, you work that much harder at doing an even better job.

True, the smiles of encouragement don't make the same loud noises that the demons and monsters do, but they are powerful. They come in the phone call that you know is genuine. "Pastor, I was just praying for you, and I wanted you to know I appreciate what you are doing." Or, "Pastor, in your sermon, you said…That really spoke to me. Don't give up!"

Sometimes that encouragement comes when you really need it. God directs someone to call you and give you some words that will pick you up in those difficult times, the dark times, your "valleys of the shadow of death," when you are in the midst of growling, sneering monsters. God will cause you to sit at a banquet table, eat, and fellowship with Him in full view of the monsters in your life. Non believers and others Christians struggling in the faith need to see you overcome. Because He is a loving God, I believe that He does that with the hope of turning monsters into saints, if conviction is able to set in on them.

Recently, God gave me a sermon from Psalm 139 entitled "Because I Am Fearfully and Wonderfully Made." I made the statement, "When you get kicked to the curb, God will pick you up and use that curb as your stepping-stone to your next level of blessing." There is just no better way to put it.

In all that Joseph went through because of his jealous brothers, at the end of his trial when they came to him, he said, "Everything you meant for my destruction, God has used for my good." Had Joseph not been in Egypt, he would not have been in the position to be a blessing to his family and the nation. There are times when God uses even our mess-ups as our next steps up or out of our pain. Even then, we gain something for Him. No cross, no crown.)

Encouragement comes because someone values what God has given you to impart to him or her and to speak blessings, strength, and healing into his or her life. The encouragers usually see and hear what is going on around you but do not buy into the negativity. The encouragers are those who are hungry to grow in the Lord. They will pray for you. You can count on them not to play into any undercurrents or negativity stirred up by nonspiritual people in the congregation. Now, I don't claim to be an expert in these matters. I can only go by what I have observed over the years in many different church settings, denominations, and denominational organizations. The bottom line is that when people are not Christ centered, they take a worldly approach to matters of how a church should operate, what a pastor should or should not do, who should be in charge, and who should lead. It is never about Christ for them.

No pastor should ever have to endure this, but many do. It is clearly not of God, not Biblically correct, not Christlike, and not worth dignifying by wasting your time and energy on. I have seen this happen in many situations across the country over the years. Postcards and letters are sent to churches anonymously so that one person can highlight his or her issue(s). Anonymous letters are sent to pastors, voicing displeasure or making outright threats. There are two ways to deal with this ungodly behavior.

First, churches, conferences, conventions, and associations should never dignify anything anonymous. If the author is too ungodly and cowardly to sign his or her name to what he or she had to say, then it is not worth your time and effort to address. The scripture tells us to go to the brother (or sister) we have an issue with and discuss the matter.

Second, since September 11, 2001, using the US mail to harass and threaten people is taken a lot more seriously, and it can be treated as a criminal matter. If you know who has done these things, fellowship needs to be severed. They mean the church no good. Remember that monsters desire to breed more monsters. There is no place for that in the family of Christ.

The Teachable and the Unteachable

One of the greatest joys of being a pastor is what a teacher sees in a classroom. That is the joy of seeing someone come into a new revelation and new knowledge from what you have shared. What excitement that brings. I remember working with a little boy at Woodridge Elementary School in Prince George's County, Maryland. He was a first-grade student who, near the end of the year, was still having trouble recognizing words he should have known in kindergarten. I volunteered to work with him one-on-one during his time with me in the library. Each day, I would try to help him learn basic words, such as *the, big, little, am, is, are,* and several nouns that he should have known by that time. He would bring his reading book to me, and as I worked with him, I had to tell him just about every word on the page. If I told him the word, he would not recognize the same word in the next line. I started writing down the words he knew and made little cards with those words. Then I made cards with the words he did not know.

God spoke to me in that library one morning, saying, "Don't open the reading book this morning; ask him about the things he likes." I did that, and he started talking about my hobby, trains, and Teenage Mutant Ninja Turtles. I wrote down the sentences he used, cut the words out, and then set them in front of him. As he started to struggle with the first word, something clicked for him when he recognized what he was seeing were his words that had just come from his mouth. His face lit up. With tears in his eyes, he yelled, "Mr. Jackson, I'm reading!"

I hugged him and said, "Yes, you are! Yes, you are!" We spent the next hour shuffling words on the table and making up sentences. He was as excited as I was. We had to call the principal and show his classroom teacher. His teacher and I had a hard time fighting back tears as we saw the joy of this little boy's discovery—the joy of reading.

That is the same joy I experience when I see believers come to know Christ, come into a new truth from God's word, or gain a new level of strength and victory because of what God has given them. When God gives you a word or a concept to bless His people, a peaceful anointing comes over you that is indescribable. It makes you want to dig as deeply as you possibly can to glean from His word to feed the people of God. However, not everyone in your ministry will appreciate what God has given you. There will always be some who feel that you cannot teach them anything. They will refuse to sit under your teaching no matter what, yet they will not leave and go where they do believe in the teaching of the pastor. They will find excuses not to attend workshops you facilitate, Bible studies you conduct, and leadership training you coordinate, deeming them unimportant or unnecessary. They may even say, "Oh, I had that before" at this place or that, under Reverend Y or Dr. X. I don't need that from him or her.

Anytime people refuse teaching from the pastor of the church they attend, they should find another church or acknowledge the fact that they are in sin for rejecting teaching from the servant of God over that branch of Zion. This is something that grieves my heart greatly.

Preaching in Season and out of Season
Preaching is a gift and a passion that carries with it a tremendous anointing. It should always be taken seriously, prayerfully, and with a sincere desire to reach others with the message of salvation, healing, deliverance, and exhortation. Paul told Timothy in 2 Timothy 4:2 to, "Preach the word; be instant in season, out of season; reprove rebuke, exhort with all longsuffering (patience) and doctrine."

What an awesome responsibility! What an awesome task! What a humbling honor that God chose me, a lowly sinner saved by His grace, to share His word!

Over the years, I have taken many bicycle rides, totaling several thousand miles. I led hikes while working in the National Park Service in my last two years of high school and four years of college. I have driven millions of miles in a car and as a bus operator, and several hundred miles as a volunteer streetcar motorman at trolley museums. I have ridden trains across the country several times, and I slowly have swum laps at an indoor pool. However, the longest distance I have ever traveled is from the pulpit chair to the sacred desk to deliver the word of God each Sunday. Every time I stand before the people of God to deliver the word He has placed in my heart, I am reminded that it is not about me; it is all about Christ.

The "in-season preaching" is when things are going well for you and the church. In those times, I stand and take the "long walk" from chair to the sacred podium whispering to myself, "God, I am so excited for this day and this privilege to declare Your word. Let me do it in a way that truly honors You and glorifies You. Hide me behind the cross, and surround me with Your presence until I overflow with Your grace."

During these times, you feel no burden, stress, or trouble. You just know that God is there with you in the power of the Holy Ghost. This is the feeling and presence I feel most of the time when I deliver the word of God. Those are the times you feel like you could run ninety miles an hour and scream praises to God. If a mosquito were to bite in those moments, I believe the mosquito would start singing, "There's Power in the Blood!"

Then there is the "out season," of which there are two types. There is an out season when there are hurts in the people and/or in you. I can remember the first funeral for which I officiated as pastor of my church. It was a difficult funeral because the family was so distraught. The deceased woman had died suddenly with no sign of sickness. I had to pray so hard for God to give me the words to bring comfort to the family. That was thirty-four years ago, and I remember it like it happened yesterday.

The first and only funeral for a stillborn I have done was traumatic for me. I had never seen such a small casket and corpse. The casket was smaller than an ice cooler. I don't even remember what type of comforting message I gave to the family. I can only remember embracing the mother tightly as she bitterly wept in my arms before we started the service at the funeral home. For several weeks, I could only see that tiny lifeless body. I kept praying, "God, how can *You* give comfort in such a difficult situation? I could not have gotten through that without You."

I have eulogized many members of the church in my years there as pastor. However, two of them were particularly draining. The first was an elderly brother and sister who had been residing in different nursing homes. When I would visit one of them, they would ask about each other. For several years, as I served Communion to one or the other, I would always hear, "Have you seen my brother?" Or, "Have you seen my sister?" They had a closeness that could not be severed, even though they were in different nursing facilities in different counties. One day, I went to visit the brother, who asked about his sister. Later that night, he passed away. The next morning, the sister passed as well. There was a double funeral. To this day, it is the only double funeral I have done. Through giving comfort to the family, as I took the "long walk" to deliver the message, God gave me a vision of Jesus going to receive the brother, taking him along to receive his sister, and then taking them together to be with Him in Glory.

The second funeral service that stands out involved the suicide by hanging of a member who had suffered severe depression. I had visited the young man in the intensive care unit, as his attempt left him brain dead. The family labored over the decision to take him off life support. That was a difficult funeral to prepare for. I lost several nights' sleep as I labored over the thoughts of most people that suicide is self-murder and that one who commits suicide would automatically go to hell. I knew the family was dealing with the same "traditional thinking" on that. I got many phone calls from church members who were also having a hard time dealing with the suicide and the issue of whether this man was in heaven or hell. The night before the funeral, I went to sleep dreading the thought of "the long walk" to give the eulogy. I could only give comfort to the mother and siblings. That night, God spoke to me and showed me that not only could I give comfort, but I also could give the congregation the message that He showed me that night. Depression is an illness of the mind. It is a sickness that causes one to lose rational thought. God showed me that it was the illness that brought about the death. I felt in my spirit that because the man was saved, he was with the Lord. It helped us all through that difficult moment.

There is the "out season" of when you are not feeling well, or you are worried or stressed because of church drama. The "long walk" to preach gets extremely long at those times. You have to pray especially hard that you say what God wants you to say and do not throw rocks at the monsters who sit there in the congregation sucking their teeth, smirking, rolling their eyes, or giving you looks that could kill. At those times, you pray hard that God keeps you focused on Him and not on the people. It is humbling and affirming to hear in those times that the message was a blessing because you know it was not *yours* but God's. Several years ago, during a difficult period, my "out season" involved preaching through some difficult times and situations in which friends said, "I don't know how you preached through that week after week."

My answer was and is, "It's not me; it's God." I can take no credit for it at all. I just believed that God would see me through. I also found this to be true when my mother passed away and I had to preach on Sundays while my sister and I were still dealing with settling her affairs after her funeral. It was only God Who gave us strength.

The longer you are pastor of a church, the harder funerals become. You develop bonds with the people. When you have been with them at their sickbeds and during family crises, when you have been to court with them when children have gotten into trouble and laughed with them during good times, their funerals become personal to you. The beautiful thing is when you know in your heart that the deceased is saved. Then, the funeral, though sad because of losing someone, can be a celebration because you know that he or she is in the arms of Jesus. There is nothing harder than to eulogize someone whose relationship with the Lord, the church, and his or her family is not "clear." You can only give comfort to those who are left and give a message of salvation.

I attended a funeral once for a man who had lived, by Christian standards, a rather shady life. The deceased had been abusive to members of his family and to his spouse at times. The preacher who was to eulogize the person stood up and began to quote a theme from a cop reality show. "Bad boy, bad boy, what you gonna do when they come for you?"

Now, my daughter and son tell me that I do not have a "poker face." I was sitting at the pulpit and cringed. Sweat began to pour off me like rainwater. I was thinking how insensitive and cruel the preacher was. He then began to talk about the man's vicious nature, his alcoholism, and his abusive behavior. He said the man should have been saved and been baptized according to the prescribed method of that denomination for the remission of his sins. If he had, he would have the Holy Ghost and not be burning in hell. People were gasping! The family stopped grieving and began to get up and walk out. I wanted to pass out. People who knew me could see that I was having a difficult time with this person's idea of a eulogy. It was absolutely awful. I wondered how many people were turned away from hearing the gospel because of that. The wife finally got up, motioned to the funeral director, and said, "Wheel my husband out of here now! We are *done* here!" She then turned to the preacher and said, "Don't you even think about going to the cemetery to commit his body! The undertaker can do it!"

Needless to say, that funeral was a conversation topic for months. An opportunity to minister was truly missed and a family's closure was ruined. You just can't do those things, even if the deceased is someone you dislike greatly. I later found out that the preacher was a family member. I can only imagine there were some heated discussions with him later.

My grandma Graham had a saying, "If there is ever any mess, it will come up at a funeral." In this case, it sure did.

Everyone deserves to have closure for a loved one that will honor his or memory. It is not up to us to determine who is right or wrong. That is God's job. Since my mother's passing, I cannot look at funerals the same way. Every time I officiate at a funeral now, I think of when I sat in the front row, facing a casket, and the feelings I had saying good-bye to someone I held dear. There has not been a time in the ten years since her passing that I have not felt empathy for those who sit in the front row at a funeral. There is no way that I can be detached from the feelings of the family in mourning now. However, one of the most rewarding experiences that I have in ministry is giving comfort to grieving families. I have been there and know what I would want to feel, in the area of comfort, should I have to go through it again.

6

BREAKING STRONGHOLDS

There are many strongholds that can keep us bound. I want to look at a few that can wreak havoc on believers and the church. They are history/tradition, the church bully, your inner demons, and your dream killer.

I am blessed that I was never bound with the issue of addiction to controlled or illegal substances. There are several reasons for that. I have a father that I know would have taken me out of this world, and I had a mother who would have swept up the leftovers. Then there were Grandma and Granddaddy Jackson, Nana, Grandma Graham, and Aunt Belle, who prayed constantly for their grandchildren and great-great nieces and nephews. They were the elders of the Jackson family clan. There were certain expectations. You did not want to embarrass the family or shame yourself. However, there were some spiritual strongholds that I had to break and some that I am still working on. Each of us has something we will work on until we die.

I still struggle with forgiving some people for some of the things they have done or attempted to do to my family, my church, or me. I know I must forgive them. Some, I have forgiven before, and like dogs returning to their vomit, they did hurtful things again and again—and sometimes again. Jesus says we are to forgive seventy times seven. In other words, our forgiveness should be limitless. However, I believe that if I have learned someone's nature, I should not continue to put myself in situations that allow him or her the opportunity to transgress against me continually. I am learning to forgive and move on. Forgiveness, I hope to cover later.

Breaking Strongholds of History and Tradition

Strongholds are a form of bondage. I remember a dog in a neighborhood I lived in that was on a chain because he would jump the fence and run off. The chain was just long enough that he could go to the fence and start to rise up. The chain would spin him around at the neck and cause him to yelp and fall. After a week or two of this, he stopped going to the fence all together. The chain was later removed, but the dog never again went to the fence. Though the chain was gone, it had a strong hold over him for the rest of his life. He died fearful of going near the fence, even though the chain was gone. His playful spirit was destroyed, to some degree. The gleam and luster in his eyes disappeared. Strongholds in our lives rob us of our zeal, our spark, our joy, and our luster.

History and tradition can be a stronghold. I know a young man who grew up in a family where the men prided themselves on keeping a string of "girlfriends" on the side, along with a wife at home. While we were in college, he told me that his dad and his uncles would get his brother and male cousins together and brag about their girlfriends and the other children they had fathered. This caused problems for his older brother, who went through several failed marriages because of that teaching and poor role model. He told me something very profound that I never forgot. He said, "When I saw what my brother went through by believing what he was told by my uncles and dad about variety being the spice of life, I decided I had to break that hold or it would control me and my family and my future children for generations."

We see this same thing in church. A pastor comes in with a vision of what God wants for the church, but someone stands up and says five famous stronghold, traditionalist words, "We've never done this before!"

Then there is the nine-word historical phrase, "This is the only way we can do it!" There is nothing wrong with history. However, doing something in a new way with a new vision and a new determination and mind-set just may carry the church to a new level. These words are usually said by those who can only see things through organizational eyes and not through the eyes of God's move. These are people who are usually only interested in position, title, and the tradition of "what always was."

Though the message of the gospel has not changed, the way Jesus reaches people has. We can end up putting the church and ourselves in bondage and miss opportunities to reach others. This is not to say we should throw away all the old songs just because they are old. How can we tailor what we have done to meet what we can do?

I am not a fan of much of the new gospel music. I love the African American gospel music style from the 1940s, '50s, and early '60s and the common-meter style that has its roots in slavery and the Deep South and has made its way to the industrial North. If I had my way, that is what we would still be singing, accompanied by a piano, a Hammond B3 or C3 with Leslie speakers, a set of drums, and some tambourines. "Bapticostal." That's my invented word for a combination of Pentecostal and Baptist. That is the style that speaks to me. However, the younger generation is not reached by that style. The generation before me, in some cases, thought the style of church music that drew me to Christ by was "out there." I am reminded that the word of God says in 1 Corinthians 9:22, "To the weak became I as weak, that I might gain the weak: I am all things to all men, that I might by all means save some."

God's plan is always going to be to break out of old molds to reach souls for His glory.

The Stronghold of the Church Bully

You will find church bullies in every denomination, in every church. They can be male or female, rich or poor. Their claim to fame is control. It is not about anything to do with God, His word, work, or His glory. It is only about the bully's personal agenda and desires. Bullies sometimes have strongholds over whole churches, pastors, choirs, administrations, trustees, deacons, mother boards, stewards, elders, lay leaders, presiding elders, families, individuals, and even bishops. They intimidate at meetings and disrupt worship services, bringing an overbearing spirit to every gathering. We can divide them into subtypes.

The church money bully likes to hold his or her money over the church's head. These bullies feel that no one gives as much as they do, that the church needs their money to make it, so they *must* call all the shots on how the money is spent. When things don't go their way, they withhold their giving or they put a noticeably small amount in the offering, in hopes that this will keep the church from meeting its denominational assessments or make the church cave in to their desires. Churches become fearful of going against what these demons want; they often give and accept less than God's plan for them. This type of bully has not a clue that God cannot be bought off or bribed the way a lobbyist buys politicians and elections or the way one buys a bit of time with a prostitute. How dare they! I have seen every kind of vehicle go into cemeteries but Brinks, Pinkerton, and Wells Fargo armored money vehicles.

The "I've got more knowledge than you have" bully thinks that nobody in the church has as much education as he or she does or is as smart as he or she is. This bully attempts to intimidate people with his knowledge in a certain field or skill area. He delights in talking above the members' heads with words that pertain to a certain vocation rather than putting things in layman's terms. (I am so glad that Jesus never looked down on anyone other than to help him or her up—though He did look up in a tree to encourage Zacchaeus to come down so that they could go to his house for a meal.) This bully looks down on and talks down to others. This bully acts as though the members have no right to ask questions about any work of the church or how they can be part of the work. This type of bully loves to ego trip in front of the congregation, while others are made to feel small and insignificant. This type of bully can also be a preacher or pastor. That is a dangerous place for a pastor to be! I would be afraid to be a pastor of a church that I administered through fear, intimidation, and bullying. Yet there are those who do it with arrogance. That is like "womanizing the bride of Christ."

The Stronghold of Your Inner Demons
The strongholds of your inner demons can go back deep into your life, even to your childhood. I mentioned earlier some of the monsters from my childhood and school years. I have a deep hatred of bullies of any kind because of what I experienced in school. It has affected me in my adult life. When I see it as a school system employee, I am very quick to act. I found that when I was the transportation supervisor for a school system, I had to take great care not go too far in punishing students who were bullies lest I became a bully in the process. In some cases, I saw that children learned the bully behavior from parents who approved of it. I remember one father and mother who sat in my office smiling when I showed them a tape of their child's behavior on the school bus. After explaining to them that the child's behavior was a violation of the Safe Schools Act, child safety laws, and the school system's Anti-Bullying Policy as outlined in the Student Code of Conduct, their yelling and screaming response was, "It's not our fault you have a bunch of wimps and pu— in your school system!" After letting them know that the conversation was over, the child was appropriately suspended from the bus. The child was also suspended from school. The parents moved out of the county to avoid sending their child to the anger-management classes he would be required to attend.

I realized that the parents represented a type of person I had gone to school with, who thrived on making the lives of others miserable. It took everything in me to maintain a professional attitude with them. I talked to a friend, Bob Shanholtz, who took a different approach than I did. Bob said, "I just beat the crap out of them, and they never bothered me again. Then they were afraid of me."

He has an interesting theory, which is that "most bullies were abused by their parents or an older sibling, making it like a game." I had not thought of that. Maybe that was the only attention they got. That however, is still a stronghold over someone else. The anger, the resentment, the bitterness, or the hatred then consume the bully's target to the point that it controls him or her. That is the stronghold.

Several years ago, I went through a couple of situations that were carefully orchestrated by people with hidden agendas. I will not go into the particulars; they are not important. Both situations had gone on for a number of years. When they ended, they left me extremely angry and bitter because of what they had cost me emotionally, financially. I survived the situations with the help of God. However, I wanted vengeance, retaliation, and loss of jobs. I would wake up each morning and imagine these people suffering all sorts of disastrous things. I wanted she bears to eat them or lightening to strike them. I wanted to see pillar-of-salt images of them, like in the scriptures. Those things did not happen. What scared me one night was a dream that I believe God used as a warning to me.

I don't like guns, though I grew up with police officers as family members in my house, and my sister, Cynthia, is a retired Washington, DC, police officer. In this dream, I bought a couple of big-game-style weapons and opened fire on these demons. Then I said, "Now I feel better." That dream seemed so real. It scared me badly that I could even dream something like that, let alone think it. I prayed for a week for God to remove the image from my mind. I knew that I needed, first, to ask God to forgive me for my thoughts and turn those people over to him. What they had done to my family, my friends, some others, and me was wrong, but God was to judge them. That was not my place. I also knew that I had to forgive them for what they had done and that I must keep my distance from them for good. This was right around the time some kid opened fire in a school and killed people after having been bullied.

One morning, I sat in my doctor's office and the nurse took my blood pressure. She looked at me and then walked out without saying a word. The doctor came in and took my blood pressure again, asking me, "What has been going on in your life?"

With a lot of tension in my voice and some not-so-nice words, I described all of the people who had conspired and done horrible things to me and against what I stand for. He said, "So, are you going to let them cause you to have a stroke? You say these situations are over or just about over. These people are out of your life now. They are not thinking about you. Why are you letting them control you and your health? Your blood pressure is sky-high!"

At that moment, God spoke to me. He let me know that these people and situations were a stronghold over me. I needed to surrender them and the situations and let Him handle them. I realized that as long as I was holding onto thoughts of them, I was keeping God from moving me forward and blessing me with healing and victory.

My blood pressure that day was 150/110. The doctor talked to me about my children, grandchildren, swimming, and my train hobby. At the end of the appointment, he took my blood pressure again, and it had gone way down.

I knew what I had to do. I started praying daily for God to help me let go of all those hurts and surrender them to Him. It has not been easy. However, the journey is paying off. No, as I mentioned once before, I am not holding hands with those people and running down the streets singing "Kumbaya." That will never happen. However, I can move on with my life. Some of those wounds are still trying to heal. Heal they must, and heal they will.

When I first thought of writing this book almost four years ago, I had to set the project aside to lay down my severe anger, bitterness, and resentment due to several situations I had gone through. When I picked it up a year and a half ago, almost all of it had to be rewritten to erase the anger, resentment, and bitterness. The more I have written, the more strongholds have fallen, and the more healing has taken place. If this book does nothing for anyone but me, it will still be worth it in the sight of God. I pray that it will help someone else as well.

Sometimes when you think the monsters have gone for good, they arrogantly show up again just to see if they can push your buttons, steal your joy, and take you back to a place of pain and bondage. This is when you really have to pray. Satan is very cunning. He will even have others tell you that you need to pretend that nothing ever happened. If you have been bitten by a poisonous snake because you didn't see the snake coming and you survived, why you would knowingly and willingly go back to where you know the snake is waiting? I am going to forgive the snake for biting me, but I will not knowingly put myself in the position to be bitten again because I now know the nature of the snake.

I will forgive the snake for biting me and then stay away from it! That is what you have to do with some people in order to break the stronghold of their venomous, toxic bites and ways. You will find that others will see their tactics and will be cautious without you saying a word.

Strongholds in our lives can cause us to have bad dreams. They can cause us to fail to live up to our potential. They diminish our job performance, interfere with our relationships, and hinder our prayer life. In the worse cases, strongholds can cause depression and substance abuse. Why would anyone allow the demons/monsters around us to have that kind of control?

Strongholds exist in our lives because we allow them to have space in our minds. We let them control and regulate our thoughts and then enter our spirits and shape our destinies. Sometimes that happens for years. When things happen to us, and we allow those emotional scars to become infected, they fester and seep their poison into us. The poison shows up as anger at the people who hurt us and as an obsession with getting back at them, getting even with them, or seeing them get what is coming to them. That means those devils that hurt us are still in control of us.

I am not a Christian who attempts to come across as having it all together. They make most people sick in the stomach. Real people can see through those types. As a pastor, I see myself as a wounded healer. I am one who has been dinged, nicked, banged up, scarred, and sometimes left for dead because of the strongholds in my life. But thanks be to God, who has given me a survivor's spirit, and to a grandmother, who encouraged me to keep at it.

My West Coast prayer partner, Pastor David Housholder, called me early (for West Coast time) one morning to tell me the word that God had given him for me just days after I'd been struggling to let go of some of those horrible things that caused me to have that terrifying dream. He told me that while he was praying, God clearly spoke to him, telling him to call me and tell me that He (God) had given me a survivor's spirit. He followed that up with his usual question, "How can I pray for you, brother?"

At that moment, I felt and literally heard that stronghold yoke snap as we prayed for each other.

People stay in abusive situations because of strongholds. Many strongholds can be connected to abusive situations. I remember a movie called *What Ever Happened to Baby Jane*. As I think of that rather bizarre movie now, it depicted several strongholds. The story was about a relationship between two sisters who were jealous and resentful of each other. One had been a childhood star with a doll made in her likeness, and the other was a cripple who had to be cared for by her sister. The star was bitter that her acting career was cut off and no one remembered her. She was also bitter at having to take care of her crippled sister. The bitterness and resentment was the stronghold that caused her to murder someone and to mistreat and abuse her sister.

The crippled sister, on the other hand, had attempted to cause the family car to run over the movie-star sister because of the stronghold of her jealousy of her sister's film career. However, she fell out of the car and the car rolled over her instead, causing her to become paralyzed. Thus, she and her sister held strongholds on each other. The strongholds carried one sister to near death from starvation and dehydration and the other to the point of insanity and delusion.

How many couples have you seen that are abusive to each other to the point that there are trips to the hospital, yet out of fear, neither partner makes a move to leave? That's a stronghold/bondage, not love. Have you ever heard anyone say, "He/She beats me because he/she loves me"? Honey, that's *not* love! That's a stronghold! To borrow a line from the movie, *Forrest Gump*, "Run, Forrest! Run!" If there are children involved in that kind of relationship, then strongholds are created in them of insecurity, lack of trust, fear, intimidation, and anger, just to name a few. Those are not easily broken, and they can cause the children to have a misguided understanding of a relationship between a man and a woman.

One needs to be so very careful to love the person he marries the way Christ loves the church. That love involves freedom to grow, freedom to be affirmed by each other, freedom to be encouraged, and freedom to be comforted in times of trouble. Those things help to minimize the possibilities of strongholds.

My daughter Melanie and I often quote lines from the movie, *The Color Purple*, produced by Oprah Winfrey. I greatly admire her for overcoming the strongholds and monsters in her life to become the woman she is today and for the way she has helped so many others to overcome strongholds in their lives. Near the end of *The Color Purple*, Miss Ceilie (Whoopi Goldberg), and Sophia (Oprah Winfrey) overcome strongholds at the dinner table in Mister's house. Miss Ceilie overcomes hers as she stands up to Mister, refusing to take anymore abuse from him. Sophia snaps out of her depressed, withdrawn state and laughs at what Miss Ceilie says to Mister. Then she says, "Sophia's home now; pass them peas!" For me, that was very moving and powerful. Then, she breaks free and gets in the rumble seat of Shug Avery's car and says, "I may be poor, I may be black, I may be ugly, but I'm here!" I admire both actors for the strongholds they broke in their personal lives. That is such an inspiration to so many.

Tyler Perry, in his Madea movies, shows how people can overcome and break strongholds. I admire him for the personal strongholds he has overcome in his life. Plus, Tyler Perry likes trains too.

Sometimes we can allow our children to be strongholds. (This is in no way a reflection on either of my children. I need to make that clear.) We all love our children and will do anything we can for them, within reason. There are situations where grown children take advantage of their parents. That is a stronghold. Yes, families should stick together. However, never, ever take advantage of each other. We should never take each other on guilt trips for what happened in the past. Talk it through, bring healing to each other where possible, and move on.

As I've mentioned, my hobby is trains. Growing up, my sister, Cynthia, always wanted to share that with me, but I would not let her. I was very protective of that all-but-sacred space of mine. It was my "alone" space, my safe space, my happy place, and my retreat from the world. Years later, she told me how much she resented me for shutting her out. She learned to hate my hobby and my passion for trains.

While we were having one of our many deep and revealing, heart-to-heart, and "tell-all-secrets-that-we-will-take-to-our-grave" sessions, I shared with her why those trains were hands-off. I told her of some of the deep wounds that I had suffered in school at the hands of people I trusted, in our neighborhood, and sometimes at the hands of "church-goers." The trains carried my mind to faraway places, where monsters could not hurt me. They carried me to make believe-worlds where I was always safe, calm, and happy. She reminded me of how I came to her rescue and snatched her from the claws of a dark monster in her life—a monster that I had blocked from my life by going down to the basement at home and running my trains for hours. That day as we shared, I picked up the engine of the train I was running on the tracks and told her to hold out her hands. At first, she said no. We were now middle-aged adults with children (grandchildren had not yet come on the scene). I grabbed her by the arm and said, "No, we have to do this for both our sakes. We can't get our healing unless we do!"

She took the engine in her hands. I said, "Hold it until you feel vindicated and justified." When she gave it back to me, I placed it on the track and said, "Now, here's the throttle. *You* run it."

At that moment, that stronghold was broken between us. Now, when she calls me with a question about a train she has seen, she usually says something like, "Why am I looking at and noticing all these trains and whistle and horn sounds now?"

I always jokingly yet seriously say, "Thank you, Jesus! She's been healed! She's been reconciled!"

Her response is joking. "You are so silly!" We then both laugh. What is so amazing is that we, who scrapped like cats and dogs as children, are now inseparable in the spirit. I led her to the Lord, preached her ordination sermon, and we affirm each other in our ministries as we encourage each other. Oh, how that stronghold has broken!

She now lives near railroad tracks—along a line that also passes near me, five hours to the east. She calls me sometimes at night and says, "I just heard this train moving really slowly, but it sounded like it had engines on both ends."

"Oh, that's a coal drag going west with helpers on the rear. It passed here four hours ago," I say. Or, "That's the passenger train you heard at 5:30 a.m. It will be here around noon, if it's not late." That stronghold is now gone for good.

She says, "Trains are not my hobby, but I now know a lot about them." Satan can never again use that as a wedge between us. For me, trains are no longer just an escape but a passion that I also use as a tool for ministry. I thank God that I have had several opportunities to use trains as a doorway to witness and lead people to Christ and to help others break some strongholds in their lives. I am now free to enjoy it as a hobby, a way to relax and to be creative.

The Stronghold of Your Dream Killer
Something I learned a long time ago is that you can't share your dream with everyone. There are some people whose purpose in life is to put down everything someone else does. Watch out for those who criticize your hobbies, your passions, and your dreams. Those things are a part of who you are. Once, when someone in my family was

writing something, I overheard someone else laugh and say on the telephone, "They call themselves writing a book." The writer was extremely hurt by that and did not write anymore for years. How hurtful! How discouraging! How demeaning! Put-downs that sink into your spirit are strongholds. They are worse than a cancer. They slowly kill who and what you could become.

I remember the guidance counselor who, when I said that I wanted to go to college, told me that the best I could hope for was to be a "grease monkey." I'd scored well on a test showing an understanding of how gears and machines worked. Why wouldn't I? Trains were my hobby. This was the 1960s. I learned later that this guidance counselor did not expect any African Americans to want to change from a general track to a college-prep track. Did I have to jump through extra hoops and go to summer school? Yes! Did I struggle? Yes! Did I make it? Yes! I had to keep at it!

Writing this book is not easy. It has been a four-year project that involved a great deal of work, prayer, and thought. I have only shared what I am doing with a handful of very close people because I refuse to be bombarded with negative comments about what others think I should not do, what I don't know, what I have or have not experienced, or who would benefit from what I have to say. Many times, people who kill dreams have no dreams. Or their dreams died, and they want yours to die too. As I was growing up, when my cousins from Youngstown would come to visit in DC, we would always go to the Seventh Street Wharf in Southwest and get several bushels of crabs to take home and steam. I noticed that if you used tongs to pull a crab from the basket and put it into the pot, the other crabs would grab it and pull on it to keep it in the basket. They would literally take off claws and legs in their attempt to keep it in the basket. There are people like that. They will do whatever it takes to keep you in bondage or to keep you from rising up above where you are. The friends have I talked to about this book have all agreed to say nothing until it is done. My mother had a phrase, "Never let your left hand know what your right hand is doing." I know what that means now. I know there are some people who would laugh at the fact that I am writing. Some would be extremely negative, saying things like, "He should be doing this or that, but instead, he is wasting his time writing what he thinks will be a book."

So, when you know there are people who would love to plan your life and your dreams, don't share them. I have become very guarded about my "me time" in my hobby, my personal-growth time in study, and my enrichment time in this endeavor. People tend to criticize what they don't understand or view as a threat. Dreams and hopes are fertilized from the lips and lives of positive and encouraging people. Affirming people breathe into the lives of each other, and strongholds don't grow there.

I shared with Dr. James Harrison, the new executive minister of American Baptist Churches of the South, that I was working on this writing project, and I was thankful for the encouragement I received from him. It was as if he saw book-signing potential. I struggled through several of these chapters, laboring for over a year on the previous one. Yet in his words, I heard those familiar words from my junior high school days long ago. I head Grandma Graham saying, "Keep at it." Dr. Harrison has on several occasions encouraged me to keep at it during difficult times.

I am not going to get into a political discussion, but politics and political issues and hot topics can be strongholds. There are many things that people are passionate about these days. This has always been and always will be. I only listen to the news in little snippets so as not to allow myself to become angry at what I hear and see. When I took journalism in college, I learned that a good journalist collects the honest facts and reports them. The only time a commentator gives his or her personal views is at the end of the program or in the section of the paper called "editorial." That does not happen these days. There is no more neutral reporting. It is a lost art. It is like the "yellow journalism" of the 1920s and '30s. In my opinion, it has fueled hatred, division, and distortions of truth on all sides. I don't need anyone to tell me what and how to think. Thanks be to God, I can think and decide for myself. If my decisions and ideas are wrong, I will have to live with them. I can't let the world be a stronghold over me.

Morality cannot be legislated for the world, but we can live as witnesses. Our lives will be our statements to the world. Churches often allow their buzz topics to become a stronghold to the point where they obsess over certain issues instead of focusing on the Great Commission of going out into the world to make disciples of others, not by arm-twisting but by being a living, loving witness.

Have you ever stopped to think that Jesus ministered to the sinners in love and won them as He did the woman at the well of Samaria, the disciples He chose, the woman who was caught in the act of adultery and brought to Him, and Zacchaeus? With which of them did Jesus use the approach that we sometimes use? "You are not living right, and if you don't change, you are going to hell." Not one of them. He talked with them, taught them in love, shared with them God's word, and they each made the decision to break their respective strongholds. That is what we, as Christians, should do.

I believe that we have turned some people away from Christ by the way we, as believers, have looked down our noses at them in self-righteousness or forced Christian values on a non-Christian population. I am grieved when I hear people refer to Christians as bigoted, sexist, or racist by bitter people who have been turned off by people in the church. That is not who we are as a whole. As Christians, we have a mandate from Christ to be living witnesses to win souls by our example.

There is a stronghold of judgment that exists in churches. Many don't see it because they feel that is the way they are supposed to spread the gospel. I know this statement will not appeal to the people of many churches and denominations. However, listen to the way we explain to sinners the message of Christ. For years, many churches have used the "hellfire and brimstone" approach. In the early years of the colonies, a Reformed Church preacher by the name of Jonathan Edwards preached a sermon called "Sinners in the Hands of an Angry God" (1741) That sermon talked about how God dangled sinners over hell by a thread. Edwards ended the sermon with,

> The wrath of Almighty God is now undoubtedly hanging over a great part of this congregation: Let every one fly out of Sodom: "Haste and escape for your lives, look not behind you, escape to the mountain, lest you be consumed."
> (Read the sermon at http://www.jonathan-edwards. org/Sinners.html.)

Our style of writing and speaking has changed since 1741, but has the approach of most evangelical churches really changed much since then? How many are in the church not because of a sincere love for Christ and what He has done in their lives but out of a tremendous fear of going to hell? If you are saved, why should you continue to fear hell? Does not God's word say that whom the Son (Jesus) has set free is free indeed? That tells me that I not only have blessed insurance but also "blessed assurance." Salvation is not an "I hope so" state; it is an "I *know so*" state! I wonder how many people are living for Christ in fear and not in His love. That is so tragic. That shapes how we share His word. That shapes how we minister to hurting people. That shapes how we look at those we deem to be lost. That also shapes how the world looks at us. If we are not experiencing the freedom of Christ's love, we are living under the stronghold of fear.

I am not advocating living a loose, free-for-all, foolish life. I am advocating living a Christian life free from worrying and looking over your shoulder, wondering if you are going to heaven. If you have confessed your sin, repented of your sin, and asked Christ into your life, the Bible says you are saved. (See John 3:16, Romans 3:10, 3:23, 6:22–23, 10:9, 10:11, 10:13, and 2 Corinthians 5:17.) These are scriptures I have used for years to lead people to Christ. I have done it without stressing hell and damnation and such. (Yes, I know hell is a real place. Yes, I know there is a lake of fire. However, if I lead people to Christ, then they don't need to worry about going there when they die. Resist the devil, and he will flee from you.) I stress how much God loves and desires fellowship with us. I stress the fact that His love for us is so great that He sent Jesus to pay a price that we could not pay to redeem us to Him, to restore a fellowship that was broken in the first generation of mankind. All we have to do is accept it and begin to break the strongholds of the things that have us in bondage.

Sometimes churches make it more complicated than it is. It is not we who change us; the Holy Spirit does the changing and convicting that makes us want to change and then replaces our old natures and habits with new ones that glorify Him. Does it happen overnight? No. It is a growing-in-His-grace process. We are crucified with Christ daily. Each day, a piece of our old nature (stronghold) dies, and a little more of Jesus lives in us as we learn to trust Him through His word.

Breaking strongholds involves surrounding yourself with positive things of God. Those things consist of God's word Bible study, God's people (fellowship), God's praise (worship, corporate or public), God's praise (worship, private), and communication with God (prayer). These five things in your life help to break strongholds on a daily basis. They are as important to the Christian as air, food, water, clothing, and shelter are to everyone's daily life. As you continue to grow in Christ, He gives you the strength to break each and every stronghold in your life. That happens in His time—not in the time of others, the denomination, or the church—in God's time as the Holy Spirit helps you.

Sometimes it takes years to move beyond some of your hurts and your issues. However, it is something that you must do. Some of the strongholds that hold us have deep roots. Some of the roots have branches that extend into various areas of our lives. It is not enough just to take it off at the surface.

If you remember, I shared earlier about my first day of college, when the college professor with the monster behavior said to the class, "If I like you, you'll pass; if I don't like you, you will fail." Then, he leaned into my face and asked if I caught his drift. I was one of three persons of color in the classroom and one of twenty-seven in the entire school at that time. I let that monster behavior defer my dream of teaching for years. I changed my major from education to social studies and English to avoid his classes, which were required for an education major. Had I known then what I know now, I would have taken some action that would have cost him his job or filed a discrimination lawsuit that would have really made some waves in 1969. That festered in me for years as an unfulfilled dream, leaving me bitter. It affected my performance in college, caused me to doubt what I knew, to struggle, to have mental blocks, and to resent the subject matter that he taught for decades. However, I survived and graduated from another college successfully. I deferred that dream of being in education until my daughter, Melanie, started kindergarten, and I did not want to let her go to people I did not know. I went to school with her. The only way the principal got me away from the classroom door was to put me to work. First, he made me the PTA president because nobody wanted that job. Next, he signed me up to be a Title I volunteer reader. When he found out that I had a degree, he handed me a substitute-teacher application, and for three years, I worked every day the children were in school along with working my full-time job as a bus operator and serving as a pastor at my current church. Next, I was a long-term substitute first-grade teacher, who ended up causing children's test scores to double that year. The next year, I was a long-term substitute teacher in a combined third- and fourth-grade classroom. (I was still a full-time bus operator and a pastor, by the way.) Then, for the next ten years until Melanie graduated from high school, I was an instructional media aide. The Year Melanie graduated from Prince George's County Schools in Maryland, I got a job in as a Media Specialist in Jefferson County Schools in West Virginia. That position, I held for six years. I was then approved for the position of transportation supervisor (the number-two position in the transportation department for the school system). I was the first minority person to hold that position. Since I retired, I have gone back to substitute teaching, which I still enjoy. I often smile now as I think back to that first day of college, when that professor walked away from my desk mumbling under his breath, "None of these idiots should be here." I wonder where the "idiots" to whom he was referring went. Oh, well.

By the way, Melanie is now a teacher certified in two areas of study. She is an excellent educator. I have seen her in action. (Way to go, Melanie! Don't ever let anyone tell you otherwise! This is coming from your pa!) She paid me the greatest compliment one Father's Day, and I shall never forget it.

> Daddy, you were mean and surly! You dragged me to church, conventions, followed me to school, substituted in my classroom, were my librarian, and took no foolishness in class, but you were fair. You took me on train trips, bike rides, and I watched you study. I blame you for my career in teaching. Now, I am mean and surly just like you. I take no foolishness, I am fair and have good classroom-management skills. Happy Father's Day! I love you!

That same Father's Day, my son, Daniel, gave me a card in which he wrote, "You accepted me when no one else would. You gave me a family when others rejected me. Though I have sometimes caused you heartache and pain, you still love me. I am proud to be your son. I love you, Dad. Happy Father's Day!"

Daniel's adoption was finalized when he was seventeen. He had come to me horrifically scarred by many horrible monsters. May God deal with each and every one of them in due season. I don't think he will mind me telling you that he now hopes to work with me in a ministry to help others heal from the hurt caused by the monsters in their lives.

I will go to my grave with that vindication for my first day of college (now forty-eight years ago) etched in my mind from the lips of my beloved daughter. I still plan to get certified in some area of education, even if I never use it or only use it for a day, just to know that even in my now senior years, I have done it. Yes, I plan to keep at it.

I recently saw a Facebook post by a cousin, who stated the names of people who were told they would not amount to anything or that their dreams should be set aside, yet who achieved success. I think of how I had to take reading courses in college because I read poorly and slowly. Yet one day, while taking a master's-level Special Education course, I read the characteristics of a learning disability and realized that what I had in grade school, junior high, high school, and college was a learning disability that was never diagnosed. Educators didn't do that back in the "dark ages." My eyes had trouble focusing on the words on a page. I learned on my own to compensate by using a highlighter. As I was reading the textbook and saw some of the characteristics of a learning-disabled child, I was so excited that I called my mother on the phone and said, "Mom, I want you to think back to my fifth-grade year. Do you remember anything about it?"

"Oh, yes," she said. "You struggled. The teacher said you had a high IQ but were lazy because you would not focus."

I told her, "Mom, I want you to listen to this." I read to her the section on some of the characteristics of learning disabilities.

When I finished, she said, "Oh, my God! That describes you to a T. I wish we had known."

"There was no way you could have known," I said. "I learned to compensate on my own. No one was diagnosing it then." For me, another stronghold was broken! A stigma was gone for good. To this day, I still study with a highlighter (preferably yellow) close at hand. All my Bibles are marked. My own copies of books are usually marked. I also teach and preach the way I learn, using analogies and comparisons. If I have no hook to hang it on and compare it with, I can't learn it. You will notice that I have used that same technique throughout this writing. If I should ever do something like this again, I will probably do the same thing. It helps break strongholds for me, and I figure there must be someone out there who needs the same approach.

Letting someone keep a stronghold like that over you is like sustaining an injury or having a severe infection that does not want to heal. Sometimes, seeing the people/monsters, being in the place where a hurt took place, or seeing something that reminds you of the monsters or situations that caused you pain brings hurts that you thought were healed back to the surface again. The infection has gone deep enough that you need wound therapy. In the medical sense, I believe that is when a doctor must irrigate your wound, perhaps removing dead skin or grafting new skin, and treat you with heavy doses of antibiotics.

That is also what happens in the spirit. Sometimes Satan brings those things (monsters) back in your face, causing you to slip back into that bitter place, that angry place, or those fresh, remembering places of the pain that was caused to you. That is when you have to ask Him to wash those wounds fresh with the "blood of Jesus" and graft new creation skin over them. You must ask God to take those places away from the depths of your heart so that they will no longer spread their effects throughout your being. It takes a while to realize that when people say and do hurtful things to you, it is not about you; a deficiency in *them* makes them feel the need to tear someone else down in order to build themselves up. The way you get beyond it is to build yourself up in God's word and live on His promises as to who and what you are. Start with something like Psalm 139:14, "I will praise thee; for I am fearfully and wonderfully made; marvelous are Thy works; and that my soul knoweth right well."

Galatians 5:1 says, "Stand fast therefore in the liberty wherewith Christ hath made us free, and be not entangled again with the yoke of bondage." (That is referring to strongholds.)

This means we must stand firm in our thoughts, our dreams, our visions, our passions, and our hopes for the future and what we hope to become.

There are so many promises in the Bible about who we are in the Lord. You can do a word study on the promise of God or affirmations as to who we are in Christ or the like. You will find many powerful verses that will affirm you in your faith.

When negativity pops up in your life, take a step back, imagine there is a warning alarm going off in your spirit, and tell yourself that with God's help you will not let the negativity control you and your destiny in the Lord. Pray and ask God to guide you through each storm. Storms will come, but Jesus has authority over storms and can walk on the choppy waters of your life and declare "peace be still." When the strongholds of your storms are broken, you gain a testimony of victory. You gain strength. When you gain that strength, nothing and no one can take it from you. It becomes a part of you, your nature, and your character.

7

THERE WILL ALWAYS BE STORMS

Lessons Learned in Storms

Let me start this section by explaining something about storms that I have found somewhat indigenous to African Americans. I was taught from a very early age that when a thunderstorm started, you turned off the televisions, record players, electric trains, irons, washing machines, and any other appliances and sat quietly in the front room or family room. The lights were off. You just sat there together quietly until the storm passed. I don't care whom I talk to in my age bracket or older, they were raised the same way. My grand-mothers would say either that God was working or that He was in His fury. If it happened in the middle of the night, you just lay in your bed, not making a sound, and you were told to pray. One thing that is certain is that there will always be storms. Some storms will be worse than others. Some will be quick storms, and some will move over us slowly and painfully. Some storms cause little damage, while others are devastating.

When I think on it now, it was as if during storms, you were to rally together and draw strength and comfort from each other. That is what happens when a loved one is near death or passes, and fami-lies come together. They cry with each other, share memories, they laugh a little, and they laugh and cry sometimes in the same breath.

What stands out is the fact that everyone is together during a stormy time—the storm of the loss of a loved one.

I vaguely remember Grandma Jackson's brother, John Grant (Uncle John) being sick. He was at home, lying in bed, and we had made the journey from Washington, DC, to Rectortown, Virginia, to see him and to spend time with the family. That was always a happy time for me, as I mentioned earlier. I can see him now, lying in bed with his eyes closed. At five or six years old, I did not know that he was near death. I remember my grandmother standing there, looking at her brother, with my grandfather standing next to her. Granddaddy was holding Grandma as I had never seen him hold her before. Neither of them said a word; they just stood there. My grandmother reached over and put her hand on Uncle John's hand. I saw Uncle John close his hand ever so gently on my grandmother's hand as he opened his eyes, turned, and looked at her.

"Yes, John," she said, "it's Rebecca and Walter." She put her hand on his forehead, kissed his cheek, turned, and walked away with Granddaddy holding her by the arm. There were tears in her eyes. This was an emotion I did not understand. Rectortown always brought smiles to Grandma and Granddaddy, as well as to the rest of us. They were not smiling. I believe that was the last time Grandma saw Uncle John alive. We went back to Rectortown the next week. This time, it was for his funeral. Most of the children stayed at Cousin Foster and Cousin Virginia's house. I remember being in my play clothes. When the adults came back from the funeral, there was a somber tone to the gathering, instead of the usual. There is always some humor, even in the saddest moments. I remember hearing the grown folks laughing about some woman who, at the graveside, was so grief stricken that as the body was being lowered into the ground, she yelled, "Oh, Lord! My meal ticket is gone!"

As I remember the story, the woman was screaming, "Let me go! Oh, let me go!" as relatives were holding her back from the edge of the grave. Then, someone in the back yelled, "Turn her loose!"

At that moment, as her feet curled over the edge of the grave, the woman stopped grieving and crying, and she dug her heals in to keep from following the casket down into the six-foot-deep grave.

Now, remember, I was overhearing this at five or six years old, and I heard this story many times after that. It always invoked laughter from family members. My ninety-three year old father filled in some of the particulars for me, such as who she was and what the circumstances were. (Uncle John's first wife had passed years earlier. So this was a second wife and not the mother of his children.) Even in the midst of the storms of grief, there is humor, as you will see. Sometimes you laugh and cry at the same time.

Even though there had been laughter about the graveside incident, there was still a great sense of loss for the family. Finding something to laugh about during a storm of sorrow and grief helps you weather the storm (ride it out) as you draw strength to make it through each day with God's grace. Grandma Jackson would have her quiet moments during the following days as she worked around her house. I now know that she was reflecting on the life of her brother. I remember how close she seemed to be to Uncle Rob, who was her last sibling. I will never forget one Homecoming Sunday at Mount Olive Baptist in Rectortown, how glad she was to be there with her brother, Deacon Robert Grant. She reached out to him at the service, held his hand, and said, "It's just the two of us left now. The rest are gone." I remember thinking that it is important to cherish the moments we have here with our loved ones.

Fortunately, funerals were spaced out in my family for a long time. I don't remember another major event of this nature until Grandma Graham got a phone call that her brother, Uncle Rufus Myree, had passed in Cleveland, Ohio. He had been a singer in several gospel groups in and around Cleveland. Uncle Rufus was very tall. He was seven foot one. He had to have his cars specially adjusted so that he could push the driver's seat back far enough to sit and drive comfortably. He had to stoop to get through all doorways. All of Grandma Graham's brothers were tall, and Uncle Rufus was the tallest. When he passed, a special casket had to be ordered. I vaguely remember my great-aunt fussing about how the cemetery had dug the grave too short and ordered a vault too short for the casket and had to send it back and get a longer one. Oh, was she angry, fussing about how she was sick and tired of the trips she had made by train and streetcar to get that all straightened out.

I remember that funeral in early January 1962 well because my grandmother, mother, sister, and I went from DC to Youngstown on the B&O train. My sister and I stayed at Uncle Morris and Aunt Katie's home with our cousins (their children) Donald, Nancy, and Kenny, while Grandma and Momma stayed with Uncle Louis and Aunt Cinnie before the funeral. The trip stuck in my mind because of the train ride to and from Youngstown. The scenery was breathtaking. I did not want that trip to end. I knew I was going to my great-uncle's funeral, but there was a peace and excitement about being out of school to take this trip in my sixth-grade year. I hung on every clickety-clack of the tracks. This was the same rail line that passed near my classroom windows and that I could also see from my parent's bedroom window on First Place NE, about a mile up the tracks from the school. Now I was on that line, on one of the trains that I would often hear in school and daydream about riding to Youngstown and beyond. Now I was on it. (Who would have thought that thirty-three years later, I would move to West Virginia and live alongside that same line.) Trains were—and still are—a safe haven during my storms, even when I pray. When I pray, I always imagine that Jesus comes into my prayer time and takes a long-distance train ride while I talk with Him.

I remember at the viewing (in Youngstown and Cleveland, viewings are referred to as "calling hours"), standing next to my grandmother as she looked down at Uncle Rufus. She did not shed a tear or make a sound. Why I remember that dark cherrywood, full couch-type casket, Uncle Rufus's charcoal gray-black suit, the red velvet throw over his lower body, and the white gloves on his hands, I don't know. I thought to myself, "Why aren't his feet sticking up under the velvet blanket?" I remember, as does my sister, Cynthia, how my grandma Graham wanted to raise the blanket to see what the undertaker had done to her brother's feet. Someone kept pleading with her not to raise it to look. I was so tempted to pick it up and look. I knew that I had better not. I remember that as we rode back to Youngstown, there was a big discussion about what had happened to Uncle Rufus's feet. We will never know. That will remain an unsolved mystery.

The funeral the next day was like a gospel concert—every gospel group for miles around sang. There was some good and lively singing. I kept thinking that heaven must be like this. It did not really seem like a sad event, except for my great-aunt, who cried out occasionally. It must have been the longest funeral I have ever witnessed in my life, but it was mostly gospel music and a short eulogy. The church was packed. I saw strength in my grandma Graham as I had never seen before. I don't remember seeing her shed a tear. She rode that storm of grief with great courage. I knew that she knew she would see her brother again at the feet of Jesus.

This was a witness to me in two ways. It showed me that your grief can be strong to the point of being overpowering and yet there is comfort in knowing that if you are in Christ, you will see your precious loved one again at the feet of Jesus. Grandma's strength to go through the storm of her grief did not come from an earthly source; it came from a very strong committed relationship to Christ. Years later, I would understand on a more personal level. (I will get to that a little later.)

We had a temporary reprieve from experiencing the death of any close family members. We went from 1962 to 1967, when Nana went to be with Jesus. I vividly remember thinking, Granddaddy's mother—and Aunt Ethel and Aunt Susie's mother—is gone! My grandfather won't get to wear a red carnation on Mother's Day anymore! Uncle Benny (my grandfather's uncle) and Aunt Belle's sister is gone! My father and my aunt no longer have their grandmother! This was my great-grandmother! How will this affect our family?

I didn't like the feeling. Death is not comfortable. It is painful, stressful, and seemingly final. Death disrupts your life tremendously. *Death doesn't play fair!* It is like getting punched in the stomach by someone a hundred times your size, and you can't fight back. Yes, I know Nana was ninety-three years old and had what today would be called dementia (then it was senility). However, she was our Nana! We loved her, and were going to miss her.

I thought of all those times I'd laughed at Nana and Grandma Jackson watching wrestling and egging on Bobo Brazil. I thought of the days when she would call and tell Grandma Jackson to have me walk to the corner store, get some table cream, sugar, and a loaf of Wonder Bread, and deliver it to her. She would always give me a dime, or on good days, a whole quarter! I always felt rich back then in the mid-1950s.

As I stood looking down at her lifeless body in the gray casket, I remembered how, when I asked her what sound her wringer washing machine made, she always said, "It says, 'Mind your own business, mind your own business.'" I would always laugh. To this day, when I walk into my dad's house (he now owns Nana's house), I still imagine her washing clothes in the basement on Monday and ironing on Tuesday. I know she would be happy that her ninety three year-old grandson (my dad) has kept her house.

Nana's funeral was hard. Aunt Belle had a nurse with her because she had a tendency to faint, to say the least. That kept everyone upset. The viewing had been at Aunt Ethel and Aunt Susie's house. Nana rested in state in the living room. I will never forget how Aunt Belle walked in the day of the funeral, before we left for Metropolitan Baptist Church. She leaned down, looked in Nana's face, stood up, and then, as my dad ran up behind her, she fainted clean away. My dad and Cousin Vernon caught her as everyone cleared a path to the sofa. They carried her there, and the nurse administered smelling salts. I thought, "Oh, boy, here we go." From that point on, there were tissues flying, and snorting and snottin' going on all the way through the funeral to Lincoln Cemetery, just across the DC line on Suitland Avenue in Maryland. Aside from the humor of Aunt Belle's reactions at Nana's funeral, there was something about the loss of Nana that none of us would ever get over. The storm of that loss was devastating for my grandfather and great-aunts. Though Nana was ninety-three years old, my grandfather and great-aunts had lost their mother; my father and aunt had lost their grandmother; my great-great aunt (Aunt Belle) had lost her oldest sibling. The Jackson family's senior matriarch was dead. Aunt Belle was held in high regard as the sister of the late matriarch, and she was loved as Nana had been loved. However, Grandma and Granddaddy became the undisputed patriarch and matriarch of the Jackson family. Death changes things. A chapter in the life of the family was now closed.

We, as a family, would get a reprieve from death until November 1970, when my oldest cousin, Vernon, was murdered a few days before Thanksgiving. That was the most devastating thing we had experienced as a family. Vernon was only twenty-eight years old—eight years my senior and four years younger than my uncle Glenn.

There was deep hurt, anger, resentment, depression, and worry about Grandma Jackson's heart condition. She had lost her oldest grandchild senselessly. We held his funeral the day before Thanksgiving. I remember that Vernon's body was brought to Grandma and Granddaddy's house. He lay in state in the living room overnight before the funeral. It is strange how these things have stayed etched in my mind. I remember the stresses, the tension, and people's reactions. Aunt Belle passed out several times during the viewing and the funeral. I remember taps being played, how we all jumped as the guns were fired, and how Vernon's girlfriend screamed his name as she was carried back to the car. I had never experienced that in person before. At every funeral since then, I have thought about that experience. Vernon's death was the catalyst that made my sister and me draw close to each other. We have been close since that time. The bond got stronger still after I led her to Christ. Death causes you to realize the importance of those close to you. Since Vernon's death, each death of a family member or very close friend has made me appreciate, cherish, and value those I hold dear. It has also taught me not to waste time and energy on hurtful, negative people who make it a point to attempt to destroy my life. I forgive them, love them at a distance, have no further dealings with them, and move on with my life.

In December 1972, death visited us again on the Graham side of the family with the sudden death of my mother's oldest sibling, Marzett (Uncle Zetty). He lived just two doors up the street from us. He had an aneurism while in Baltimore, drove himself to the hospital, and dropped dead on the floor of the lobby. What stands out for me from that experience was that I never saw my grandma Graham shed a tear the whole time. She had lost Uncle Leo as an infant. Now, Uncle Zetty, who was in his late forties. Grandma did not get out of the limousine at the cemetery. I walked up to the front limousine to see if Grandma was OK. She took my hand and began to keep time, pounding my hand on her knee as she sang,

> Be ready when He comes.
> Be ready when He comes.
> Be ready when He comes.
> He's coming again so soon.

At that point, she stopped singing. She had a radiant glow on her face that I had never seen before and the far-off look I have since seen in others preparing to "cross over" to be with Jesus. She said to me, "You know that's the truth, son." Then she went back to singing,

> Be praying when He comes.
> Be praying when He comes.
> Be praying when He comes.
> He's coming again so soon.

Somehow, even though I did not understand things of the Holy Ghost as I do now, I felt in my spirit that she was telling me in code that she was going to be next. That is another experience that has remained as fresh in my mind as the day it happened. I can see all of that in my mind, even now, ever so clearly.

On Sunday morning March 11, 1973, Grandma Graham was found in her bed. She had slipped into Jesus's arms while she slept during the night. I knew she was ready. I knew she was praying when He came so soon. It was on that same night that the Holy Ghost filled me with His divine presence and comfort and reminded me that He had told me He was coming again so soon through the song Grandma sang to me. I had peace in the midst of this storm. I had comfort and strength in the midst of the storm of her passing and the one that would follow on Tuesday November 20, 1973, just before Thanksgiving, when Grandma Jackson also went to be with Jesus. She sat down in my grandfather's chair, with one foot on the hassock and one on the floor, and fell asleep in Jesus's arms. Death takes no holidays or vacations.

These two funerals were different for me because now I knew Jesus for myself. Though sad in the flesh, I was comforted in the fact that I knew—and know—with certainty that I will see them all again at Jesus's feet. They will have glorified bodies in robes of righteousness, new names, and new songs to sing.

There were some funerals after my grandmothers', but none had a tremendous impact until June 2005. As a pastor, I have officiated at many funerals and will probably do a few more before my time is up. However, grief punched me hard in the stomach on Wednesday June 15, 2005, at 8:15 p.m., when my sister called my cell phone, saying hysterically, "Momma is lying on the kitchen floor unconscious! Gary Smithwick (who lived across the street) went to see why she didn't answer the phone about going to her doctor appointment. He went and looked in the kitchen window, and she was on the floor. He called 911."

I had just left Bible study. We had been expecting my dad's sister, who had terminal cancer, to pass. I had gone to see Auntie on my dad's birthday and taken my Labrador retriever, Lady, and the eight puppies she had recently had to show my dad the one that was to be his, a chocolate Labrador retriever that he named Coco. Something told me to make sure to stop and see my mother. Part of me was saying, "Stop another time. This is the visit to say good-bye to your aunt, who is dying, and to comfort your dad." But I felt a strong urge to see my mother too. It was an urge I can't really explain. Even though I was pressed for time, I *knew* I had to go right then. That was Friday May 27, 2005. I must have stayed with her for over an hour. She kept saying, "I know you need to go see your father." I just kept sitting there, talking with her, while she held one of the puppies (Queenie), and Lady laid her head on my mother's leg. That was that best visit we had ever had, and it was the last time I saw Momma alive.

She kept sending me away, but I could not leave. I now know why. The Holy Spirit was giving me some farewell time with my mother! She stood at the door, waved, and watched me drive away for the last time. On June 15, she was gone.

Auntie died June 20. My birthday was June 21. We buried my mother June 22. I can't look at my birthday in the same way anymore. I sat on my front porch the next Sunday morning as God ministered to me. At that time, I was fifty-five years old. I thought about how fast fifty-five years had gone by. I thought about some of the years I had taken for granted, relationships I had taken for granted, and how others do the same. I thought of the people who are meaningful in my life. It hit me that "*life is too short not to cherish every moment you have with those you love and who are meaningful in your life!*"

When I went to identify my mother's body at the DC morgue, the attendant came out and talked to my father and me to prepare me for what I was about to see (a Polaroid-type snapshot of my mother's face, a white sheet covering her to the neck). I was to print her full name on the back of the picture and sign my name under it. The attendant talked to me about the stages of grief and gave me a pamphlet about them. It mentioned how grief will change you. It does, and it did.

It hit me that you can't waste time on idleness. You can't waste time on people of ill will because they steal precious energy and time.

Let them go, move on, surround yourself with those who love you and those you love. With a sense of urgency, you should make a difference in someone's life, because positive, loving people made a difference in yours. Ignore and block out demonic people and their antics. They are setbacks, stumbling blocks, and, yes, strongholds.

That is what my mother's death taught me. Ever since then, all I want to do is leave a legacy of love for my family, a legacy of making a difference in some small way in this big, sinful world, and leave some hope for those who may otherwise be hopeless. If in my ministry I can do that, then I will have done my job. Though I will never be famous (that's not important), making a positive, meaningful mark in the world for Christ makes life more beautiful for others.

I have preached many funerals. However, since my mother's and my aunt's deaths five days apart, I have a different perspective on death and grieving. Every time I stand to eulogize a member of my church or a family member, I relive that time between Wednesday June 15, 2005, (the date of my mother's passing) and Monday June 27, 2005, (the date of my aunt's funeral). The empathy I feel for the grieving families is intense. It is sometimes painful again. However, I thank God that I also remember how Christ got me through it.

On Christmas 2015, as I placed three flowers on my mother's grave, I thought, *Oh, what conversations we will have at the feet of Jesus!*

There will always be storms like death, heartache, disappointment, and plots against you by those you trusted in naïveté. There will be those who hate you for no reason other than you don't look like them, don't have wealth or education like theirs, don't have faith and beliefs like theirs, or because they are jealous of what God is doing in you.

There will even be racists within your own race who will have hatred for you because your complexion is darker or lighter than theirs are. This is referred to as being "color struck." For black Americans, this has roots deep within slavery, and vestiges of it hang on even to this day—thankfully, not to the level it did in my childhood. It has left deep scars of self-hatred, low self-esteem, and lost job opportunities for some. It has led to abusive behavior, and it plays out in churches, schools, and in the workplace. This is a major storm from which many still bear damage and scars. I could devote a whole book to the damage done in schools by teachers to students and students to students, by churches to pastors and pastors to members, and by employers to employees, all because someone's complexion (not race) was either too dark or too light.

Whatever the storm you have had to survive, whatever the reason, just be the best you that God would have you be. At the end of the day, that is what He requires. Ignore your bullies and let God deal with them (and He will). They have no place in the beautiful life that God has for you and the eternity He as for you after this life. Try to ride out each storm with a song in your heart, because you are beautifully and wonderfully made in the image of a great and wonderful God. It is not your fault that others don't know it, can't accept it, or don't realize it for themselves and put you down in order to lift themselves up. I am reminded of what a pastor friend told me once. "Watch out for the ones who must always tout for you what they have, what they have done, and what they can do for you," he said. "There is something they don't feel good about that they are using all those things to compensate for." Humility needs no horns tooted for it. Greatness will be praised by others.

One of the greatest things I ever realized is that in the middle of my Bible is a hymnbook called Psalms. Some of the songs are happy songs, and some are sad. Some tell of mistakes the songwriter made and what he learned from those mistakes. I have taught my congregation this. The hymns we sing—whether they are the traditional ones of ages past that many contemporary churches consider "outdated" or "meaningless," or the contemporary stuff that seems to be popular—are *all* someone's testimony put to music, if you listen to the words! Each tells a powerful story! Each of us has our own story, no matter how great, small, joyful, sorrowful, tearful, painful, or hilarious, and one day we will sing *our new song* at Jesus' feet. We are writing it now, each and every day. Every time you share your faith story with someone, encourage someone, embrace with genuine love someone who is hurting without saying a word, *you* are singing a verse of *your* song and breathing life into his or her soul! I believe that at that point, angels fill in on harmony and sing the chorus in Heaven. The Holy Ghost adds heavenly arrangements to the song we sing and plays it back into our spirit as encouragement to keep telling our stories through our earthly storms. In doing so, we help others to weather their storms, even while we are going through ours.

I know that I will go through another storm of loss of a loved one at some point. The puppy that my mother held died November 14, 2015, ten years, six months, and two days from the day she was born. She died in the spot she was born. I was devastated. Pets are family too.

I know the next death will be painful to go through, as it has been before. I brace myself for when that day will come. I hope that when the time comes for me, my children, grandchildren, sister, and family will cherish whatever joy I gave them and love I tried to shower on them. I hope that I will have left here something of substance that will have made a tremendous difference in someone's life.

As I write this paragraph, my father's devoted friend passed away yesterday, December 30, 2015. I last saw her on Christmas Day, when I dropped off Christmas gifts to her from my dad and me and gave her a kiss on the cheek. Who would have thought that would be the last time I would see and talk to her? I will do what I can to be there for my dad, as I cherish his being here still. Each moment is precious— more precious than silver or gold. Love can't be bought. It can only be experienced and cherished.

On Saturday January 2, 2016, I received a phone call from one of my church members who informed me that her husband had just passed away. The longer you are a pastor, the more special and meaningful relationships you develop. Art (Artemus) and Deborah Arnwine's relationship reminded me so much of the relationship between my aunt Cinnie and uncle Louis. They really loved each other, and they loved the Lord, and it showed. I had gotten to know Mr.

Arnwine as a true believer who was serious about his relationship with God through conversations with him and his wife, Deborah. He was the same at home as he was at church. He reminded me so much of my uncle Louis. It was like God had given Uncle Louis back to me for a season. His spiritual personality was so much like my late uncle's that to me, he even looked like Uncle Louis, though he really didn't. However, in the spirit, he did. As I prepared for his funeral, I thought of how much Deborah loved her husband, even giving up her job as an excellent teacher to care for him for two years before his passing. I was reminded of the lessons I learned after my mother's passing, almost eleven years ago at the time of this writing. "Don't take life for granted. Don't miss an opportunity to affirm your love for you loved ones. Cherish every moment you have together. If you know Christ, the temporary hurt of the loss of your loved ones in this life will be compensated with the eternal joy of sharing joy with them in the presence of Jesus someday, for all eternity." That causes me to smile through my tears. Though I know Deborah Arnwine and her family are feeling that pain right now, I am sure she is being comforted with God's grace through this difficult time.

The Storms of Major Faith Challenges
There are times in your life when you go through challenges. Those times are not "pretty times." There was an elderly deacon at the Nineteenth Street Baptist Church (I believe it was Deacon Benjamin Thomas) whom I remember telling this story about a man who was having some serious troubles. As he was praying to God, he cried out, "Lord, I am in a big mess down here and can't see my way out of it. Lord, if You please, and if it be Your will, kindly help me through this mess. Don't send Your Son, because this mess I am in ain't no place for children!" I remember this anecdote being told as a "church joke." However, I think of this phrase as meaning a challenge to our faith. Those are the times when people or situations threaten the very fabric of what we hold true and dear in our faith, when Bible or church doctrine that we stand for is questioned, or when God takes us out of

our comfort zone into a place where we have not been or explored in Him before. Those are storms of your faith.

I have now been in ministry since 1970, when I was licensed to preach, and I was ordained in 1973. There are things I preached then that I now look at with a deeper understanding because of study, because God took me to a new level, and because negative people hoped to push personal agendas into the church and shove church doctrinal standards aside without biblical justification.

Because of the things I have studied, I now know and understand things from God's word that I did not know forty-two years ago. I read some of the sermons that I wrote when I first started preaching, and they seem shallow now, compared with what I now know. I reread scriptures that I have read many times and get a new and deeper understanding of them. I ask myself and God, "How did I not see this before?" The answer is usually, "You had not grown to the place where you could receive it."

I see some of the things that many mainline so-called conservative churches do in the name of being true to "the word of God" as being somewhat legalistic and as poor witnessing when they condemn everyone to hell who doesn't see it their way, or they attempt to force the unsaved to live by the standard for saved people. Morality cannot be legislated or mandated through the church to the unsaved world. Our job is to be a witness to the world through our lives as we let Christ live *through* us so others can see Him in us and want to follow Him. I believe we have, in many cases, become modern-day Pharisees, Sadducees, and Zealots. Instead of drawing in and making a witness, we often drive the world farther away by our approach.

If you look closely at how Jesus ministered to the world of sinners (the unsaved world of that day), He met them where they were in their dirty state, not looking down on them in self-righteousness or snobbery but with understanding, love, and compassion. He did not compromise who He is. Yet through His genuine love, He caused men and women to *want* to change and follow Him.

Did Jesus tell the woman at the well that she was a sinner and going to hell if she didn't repent and get baptized? No! He told her what He had (*living water*) and what it could and would do, and *she* made the decision to leave her water pot and tell the town to come meet the man who "told her everything about herself."

Did Jesus tell Zacchaeus that he was a reprobate and an unholy heathen who was on his way to hell? No! Instead, Jesus invited him down from the sycamore tree and invited Himself to Zacchaeus's house for dinner. Because of the way Jesus treated him and showed him compassion and love, Zacchaeus, with no arm-twisting or prompting, made the decision to give back what he had taken in overtaxation, with interest. The religious "sanctified holy folk" of that day criticized Jesus for eating with sinners. However, Jesus got results. *That* is the model the church should be following today, the one with which Jesus got results.

We could be getting the same results and still not become *like* the world. All we have to do is follow Jesus's model of soul winning and loving. He did not have to compromise the integrity and validity of the gospel to do it. Remember, He chose twelve men who were ordinary, imperfect men, some of whom had messed-up lives. He took them just as they were, taught them, and modeled the desired behavior before them for three years, and from eleven of those men and 109 more souls, on the Day of Pentecost, He started the church, and He declared, "The gates of hell shall not prevail against it!" Who are we to attempt to do things differently than the way Jesus did it, if His way works?

I know that some would say my way of thinking is "liberal doctrine." *Hardly*! I am conservative in thinking that we need to follow Jesus's example of winning people as opposed to using the fear tactics, arm-twisting, and other gimmicks. Just share your story. Honestly share what Christ has done for you. People who are lost need *your* story, shared with the love of Christ. If they don't want to hear it, it is not on you; it is on them. You just share your story with someone who will hear it. That is what Jesus did, without beating people over the head or turning the world off by trying to force it down their throats. No, I am not advocating compromising the truth of the message of Christ; I am advocating that Christians learn how to live in the joy of the Lord in such a way that people see the joy, the peace, the love, the genuine caring, the celebrating of the new life, and the compassion for others. That can be done without "stooping to walking in sin." This is where the Pharisees, Sadducees, and the religious zealots of Jesus missed the boat. They looked only at literal, legalistic interpretations of the text, even when Jesus tried to show them otherwise. They only saw what they wanted to see and believe.

God often takes us to a new level of understanding when He challenges us in our study of scripture beyond what we have been taught and takes us out of the place we are comfortable. That is a faith challenge and a storm for you. You have to work through that with sincere study and pray for guidance and understanding. Sometimes He wants to take us to another level of understanding in our faith walk. He can never take us to that new level if we are not willing to make the journey. It may take us away from what we have traditionally thought to be true. However, if Christ is leading you, be willing to make the journey.

I am going to be very candid here, and what I say may turn off some of my denominational colleagues, yet it may free others. After really understanding what it meant to have a true salvation experience on Thursday February 15, 1973, it challenged what I had understood about the concept of "joining the church." I will not say that I wasn't taught it. I will just say that my understanding up to that point was not about a commitment and a relationship with Christ. Was I sincere in what I did prior to that time? Yes. However, somehow, I never understood the commitment and the love relationship that Christ wants for us until I consciously prayed the sinner's prayer and invited Christ into my life on that Thursday night alone in my bedroom. What a different feeling came over me from deep within my being. I *knew* it was and is real. A month later, just from reading scripture, praying, and asking God privately to give me whatever He needed me to have to be equipped to preach His word to His people and to be a witness for Him the rest of my life. I knew without any doubt Christ had come into my life in a very real and personal way.

On the night I was told that Grandma Graham had passed away, I went to sing with my college choir and share the testimony of my grandmother's passing. Because I really knew Jesus, I knew I would see her again at Jesus's feet. A peace that I cannot explain came over me. After the choir sang, a group of us got together at one of the choir member's homes. They wanted to pray with me for comfort and strength. While we were praying, I heard them praying in languages I had never heard before and singing in languages I had never hear before. No one was touching me. We were all either kneeling or sitting in the family room. Having never been taught anything about the Holy Ghost—not knowing anything about Him—I took a deep breath and keeled over flat on my face, praying in a language I had never learned. I thought, "Oh, no. My grief has caused me to lose my mind." But with every part of my being, I heard the Lord speak to me and say, "You asked Me to give you what you would need to carry My word to My people. That is what I am doing. Please don't fight me. I want you to be My servant. Just trust Me."

These were not audible words but words I heard through my whole body—every part, every nerve, every cell, every hair follicle, and every skin cell. I just knew. I differ from some of my friends in other churches who understand what happened in that it was not an experience I needed to wear like a badge or flaunt in the faces of others. That was the problem (one of the problems) with the church at Corinth. I just had to let *God* use me and work through me, which He still does to this day. He speaks my sermons to me in this way! He is even speaking to me as I write these pages. It was not my desire to share this experience. I don't often share it. I just live it. A storm, for me, was the challenge of putting this experience on paper for whoever will read it. However, I make *no* apologies for what God, through Jesus Christ, has done in my life to equip me for service to Him. Everyone has to come to that place on his or her own.

I was so blessed to be praying with my aunt Cinnie and uncle Louis one Saturday night and to find that she had had the same kind of experience. I shall never forget praying that night with them in their bedroom when I went to visit them. I was scheduled to preach the next morning, and as we were praying, we all "slipped into the holy of hol-ies" as these heavenly languages started flowing. What would all these Baptist folk think of us? I really didn't care. All that mattered was that God was using all of us in the ministries in which He had placed us. I have been out of my comfort zone for forty-two years. I don't make an issue of this anointing; I just let God use me as He sees fit. I have never been led to pray aloud in the Spirit in my congregation. God is not the author of confusion. The problem with most people is that they focus on certain manifestations of the Holy Ghost rather than on the full redemptive, anointing, saving, delivering, empowering, healing, forgiving, and transforming work that God does through the person of the Holy Ghost as He equips us to live for Christ and serve Him better.

It is not about the sensations, feelings, and emotional highs. It is about making a difference in the lives of others for the cause of Christ. Yes, there are times when you are excited and filled to overflowing. However, there are also times when you are just concentrating on ministering to the needs of people to reach them with the message of Christ in a loving way. You can't always do that while dancing or experiencing your private moments of self-fulfillment.

Becoming a Spirit-filled believer was a faith-challenging storm for me in that it challenged all that I had known to be true according to traditional Baptist teaching and interpretation. Yet, as much as I loved some of the styles of worship similar to what I enjoyed of my Baptist traditions, I could not embrace fully the various Pentecostal denominational teachings and interpretations. There were certain legalistic things that just did not allow me to be free in the Lord. For me, there was too much focus on particular gifts of the Spirit rather than on the message of the gospel and the operative work of the Holy Ghost in the lives of believers. I must make it clear here that I am *not* putting down *any* denomination or its practices or beliefs. The scriptures clearly teach that each of us is to be "convinced in our own mind." How each of us chooses to worship is how we meet the Lord for ourselves. He meets us all individually as well as at collective moments when we come together on common ground. How we worship is like how we season our food. Each of us seasons it to our taste. As long as we do not compromise the *truth* of who the Lord is, He honors our worship by showing up and blessing us with His presence.

My faith storm was that He took me from a place of comfort in what I knew to a different level. It was a place where most of my family, friends, and ministerial colleagues were not. He confirmed that it was OK by letting me see that He had done this with Aunt Cinnie and Uncle Louis in their Baptist church, and He had done this with others in other Baptist churches and even at some of the conventions I've attended. I perceived, as did Peter, that God is no respecter of persons. Many, however, make the same mistake as did the people in Corinth by going into churches to "show off" their anointing in an attempt to force congregations to become like them. This is not God's way. The same God that reached you will reach them in His way and time. You just live for Jesus before them and let God do it in His way and time.

Some of my Pentecostal friends felt that I should now "come out from among them" (the Baptist) and unite with them. I was preparing for ordination at that time in 1973, and the Holy Ghost did not direct me to do so. I knew the Lord was clearly leading me to stay where I was. Again, I felt the Lord speaking to me in my being, saying, "I reached you where you are. I need you to be a light where you are." Then the verse came to me from Matthew 5:16. "Let your light so shine before men that they may see your good works and glorify your Father which is in heaven."

I knew then that I would not leave the Baptist faith unless I clearly heard from God to do so or was forced out. I would also not try to "force" any Baptist church into my experience. I believed then, as I do now, that my mission is to preach Jesus and His crucifixion under the anointing of God and with power and let God do whatever He is going to do. Some have left me because I won't force that on the church. There are friends who understand and support my approach as the Godly way to handle things. Now, forty-four years, two pastorates, and many storms later, I have no regrets for being obedient to the Lord in staying. Some would argue that maybe I have "quenched the Spirit" within me when the word of God says, "quench not the Holy Spirit." I argue that I have not quenched His operation in my ministry to the church. There have been healings, deliverances, words of knowledge, and prophetic revelations; God has revealed to me those who were at work to harm the church and how to stand against satanic attacks against His church. Not once have I had to make a big fanfare about any of the gifts God has given me; I just quietly do what needs to be done for the sake of His house. Many have had Spirit-filled moments without realizing they had gone into a different place in worship and had gently experienced the hand of God.

The Storms of Major Decisions

All of us have these storms. Sometimes they are typhoons! When you see someone who has to make the decision to take a loved one off life support when there is no living will and family members can't agree on what to do, that is a major decision storm. Someone will not be happy with the decision. Yet the decision must be made.

The storm might be the decision to leave an abusive relationship that you know God does not mean for you to endure. Many people struggle through that storm for years before they can get the peace they need with making that decision.

Have you ever had to sever a friendship because a trust was violated, a confidence compromised, or something underhanded was done to you or to your family? You had to forgive and then walk away because the trust was no longer there.

Have you ever had to use tough love on your children with an aching, trembling heart? That is a major storm.

Remember the "would-be" licensed preacher I mentioned earlier who attempted to take the church from his pastor, causing confusion in that church, destroying some baby Christians, and causing some to fall away? That was a major storm for the pastor. How difficult it must have been for that pastor to sever that tie with someone he had mentored and nurtured in ministry but now could no longer trust. The passage of scripture that comes to mind is 2 Timothy 3:8–9.

> Now Jannes and Jambres withstood Moses, so do these
> Also resist the truth: men of corrupt minds, reprobate
> concerning the faith.
> But they shall proceed no further: for their folly
> Shall be manifest unto all men, as theirs also was.

I imagine that is like having to give up a child—surrendering parental rights or burying a child. That's a hurt I imagine you just don't get over. However, you must and will move past that storm with God's help.

What about the terrible storm of having to discipline members of a church who violate a sacred trust, undermine pastoral leadership, or cause dissension in the body of Christ with no remorse? That is a major storm. Every sincere pastor has or will experienced this at some point, at some level. Some will experience it more than once. It may even cause a pastor to want to walk away. Don't *ever* take that step unless you get that *clear* direction from the Lord. God still knows how to eradicate monsters, or at least take away their fangs and neutralize their venom!

Each storm you encounter leaves some damage. The severity of the storm determines the severity of the damage and the time it will take to recover. Recovery will take place because Christ said the gates of hell will not prevail against His church—His body! The humbling thing is when He does the fixing, not you. Then you can have peace during the storm, though the storm may be difficult. There are lessons that can and will be learned through every storm. Storms also cause you to become strong. There is no place you can go to avoid life's storms. You just have to deal with them as they come. I used to wonder how and why people live in places where they have severe weather, such as tornados, hurricanes, earthquakes, flooding, forest fires, and mudslides. Then I heard someone who lives in "hurricane alley" say, "I don't know how y'all live up there with all that possibility of big snows and all that sometimes hit the Northeast. I couldn't deal with it."

Then I realized that they are used to those storms as I am used to dealing with big snows, even if I don't like them. Just as they are used to dealing with the types of storms they often face, God gives us the strength and the grace to deal with the storms we face in our lives. (I mentioned this recently in a short sermon I posted on my church's website, my Facebook page, and on the ministry website of my pastor friend and prayer partner David Housholder.) At the time of this writing, some of us in the northeastern United States are still digging out of a forty-inch snowfall.

The Storm of Sickness
Sickness and failing health are storms. Some are worse than others. I look at those who deal with cancer and chemo treatments or those who regularly undergo dialysis. Those kinds of storms take a special strength. People weather them every day; many do it with great courage. They keep smiling, though sometimes they do it through tears and great pain.

I remember when my father was diagnosed with bladder cancer not long after my grandfather passed away. My dad had been the constant caregiver for my grandfather for several years after my grandfather had repeated strokes. I remember thinking that it was so unfair for my father to have this cancer storm to deal with. There was nothing my sister or I could do to fix it. He was regularly going to the hospital for inpatient and outpatient surgery to remove cancerous tumors, yet I watched him continue to sing solos at church with great feeling and commitment of faith. He never gave up. He never let go of his faith in God. My sister and I were constantly praying, as were many others. Years later, the tumors were downgraded to noncancerous. Then one day, they were totally gone. He was in his sixties then. He is now over ninety-three. God gave him tremendous strength to weather that storm. He does have severe arthritis, uses a walker, and voluntarily stopped driving. Yet he still finds something to laugh about every day. He often has my sister and me laughing because of his sense of humor.

People who prey on senior citizens sometimes call his house. One such caller told my father that he had discovered a "bug" in his computer and could fix it for a certain price. Now, my dad does not go online; he only uses his computer to play Solitaire and a few other games. When the person on the phone told him how he could fix his computer for a "nominal fee," he told the caller, "No, that's OK. I fixed the bug myself. I've been spraying Raid down in the keyboard and killed the bug." Needless to say, the person hung up the phone. My sister and I had complete laughter meltdowns at my father's sharpness of wit. He said he looks forward to those crank calls because it gives him something to laugh about every day. (It also keeps his mind sharp.)

My sister and I have gladly made adjustments in our lives to assist him in living at home with his dog (a chocolate Labrador retriever named Coco) so that he can continue to weather his storm of arthritis pain. He says he never wants to be a grumpy old person because that cuts your life short.

The Storm of Growing Older

My grandmother used to say, "Growing old is hell." She was right. It is also another storm. When things in your body don't work as they used to, when joints pop and creak, when you hold things farther from your eyes to see them, and when you say, "Oh, Jesus," as you get in and out of a car or sit down and get up from a chair, that's a storm. When your day starts and ends not only with prayer but also with morning pills and evening pills, that's a storm! When you are on a first-name basis with your doctor and the pharmacist and you are in a love relationship with ointments to ease your pain, that's a storm. When you travel, you have a suitcase for your medicines and carry a list of everything you're taking in case you go to the hospital, that's a storm. Yet we all know that the alternative to growing old is not as pleasant and can ruin your whole day. If we are still here, it is because God is still working on us and in us. He still has things for us to do, and there are lives He still wants us to touch.

"The Storm Will Pass Over Halleu'"

When your trials of life, your obstacles, move out the way, the storm has passed, and things seem so much brighter. Have you noticed, after a severe thunderstorm, how peaceful it is? Have you noticed that the day after a big snowstorm, the sun comes out?

Each storm we go through *will* pass. We are always relieved, refreshed, and get revived. No matter how bad things look, "this too shall pass." The outcome may not be the way you want it. However, each storm passes. You will gain strength for having gone through it and survived. Never give up. You just keep at it. There is a saying, "When my ship comes in, I don't want to be at the airport." Since I hate airplanes, I would say, "When my train arrives, I will not be standing at the bus stop or driving down the highway." I want to be waiting at the appropriate place at the appropriate time.

We should always be anticipating the next big thing that God is going to do in our lives. No matter how small it may seem, we should celebrate each day and each blessing from God as a new level that He is taking us to.

Pray and ask Him to prepare you to receive that blessing at the end of each of your storms. Each storm will pass over and be gone!

8

WHEN PEACE COMES

Introduction to the Topic of Forgiveness

I owe this section to someone who is still very special in my life, though we now are apart. We are forever tied together because we raised two beautiful girls together and have some wonderful and beautiful grandchildren. Yes, I am speaking of my ex-wife, Regina Jackson. Regina and I sometimes talk and laugh together now. We had to grow to that place where we could look back on the years we spent together and remember all the good things, the fun things, and the happy things. I think that if we both knew then what we know now, things may have been different for us. Only God knows. I am sure some of you will read this chapter closely, looking for hints, clues, or whatever you can glean between the lines. However, the message of this section is about learning how to forgive.

Forgiveness

I call Regina on her birthday each year and sing her a birthday song I make up that sounds like some old-time gospel song, as I do for the rest of my family. It usually gets a laugh out of her, and she says, "Reverend, (she has always called me that) you are still silly." We laugh and talk about our grandchildren and ask about old friends and make small talk. I shared with her what I was doing, and she asked if there was a chapter on forgiveness.

"You know," I said, "That works. It will fit right in with what I have to say. You are a tremendous part of helping me get to that place of forgiveness. Thank you! May I mention you and your contribution?"

I am not going to go into the confidential conversations Regina and I have had. We have shared secrets with each other that we will each take to our graves. However, I will say that neither of us would be at the place where we are in our walks with the Lord had we not realized that forgiveness is necessary for peace and for God's plan for our lives, as Regina stated. In that healing, there came a freedom to be at peace with ourselves and each other. We can now celebrate each other in our lives, affirm each other as grandparents and parents. She encouraged me when I adopted my son. We have prayed together through different challenges that we shared and laughed about impending old-age pains. Though we don't talk daily or interfere in each other's lives, we can now relate to each other in the love of God, and she says, "Reverend, you can still make me laugh."

One day, we will be proud grandparents witnessing our grandchildren accept Christ. We claim it! Hopefully, we will live to see them marry. A few years back, my church gave me an anniversary celebration. My daughter brought her mother with her. I got up from the head table and walked to the door of the hotel ballroom, knowing that Regina doesn't like to enter late and have people stare (nor does she like crowds). I took her by the arm and escorted her to the family table by the head table, with Melanie close behind. The room went dead silent, as many of the people wondered who I was escorting in. As Regina sat down, I whispered in her ear with a straight face, "I think we will be the topic of conversation for the next week."

She responded, "Reverend, you still don't have good sense, but thank you. You know I was nervous." We had our private chuckle.

When we allow God to take us beyond our personal pain and hurt to a place of peace, we can forgive ourselves for our mistakes, and then we can forgive others. The Lord's Prayer clearly gives us the model that our forgiveness from God is tied to our ability to forgive others. You see, Regina and I have forgiven each other. I feel it deep in my heart. It does not matter what anyone else thinks. I feel that from her, and I *know* in my spirit that Regina feels it from me. Case closed!

At the request of a close friend, Elvin Bob Shanholtz, I recently visited his brother-in-law, James Tyree, in Winchester Medical Center. As it turned out, James is an American Baptist pastor, as am I. Though we had never met before, we began to see some similarities in our pastoral experiences. We had faced similar challenges, pains, attacks, and, yes, some joys. He now ministers to people in recovery. This faithful caring man of God shared something with me that stuck in my mind about forgiveness. We cannot worry about whether or not the other person accepts our forgiveness or forgives us, he said. "We have to clean *our* side of the street." That means we have to forgive others to take the weight and burden off us. That enables God to heal us and free us. I could not get that statement "clean *our* side of the street" out of my mind.

I realized that in order to be healed from a lot of the internal damage done to me and the damage that I may have caused others, a lot of my "life street" had to be swept clean. However, the only side I am responsible for cleaning is *my* side of that street. I have to keep at it until it is done, no matter how long it takes. I can't worry about what the person on the other side of the street is cleaning. In the case of Regina and me, we had both been cleaning our sides of the street. Now at times, we celebrate with a "parade of the joy of Jesus" down the middle!

I have had to clean other streets with other people and just keep walking on my side because even though I have forgiven them, I know their natures and can have no fellowship with them. In those cases, you just keep moving on in Christ.

The misconception about forgiveness is that everything has to return to the way it was before the breach in fellowship. When we mess up with God, there is always a consequence. Though He forgives us, we still pay a price for the transgression. It is like when you fall down and get up; there is still a bruise or a scar.

I have forgiven some people, yet I can never be in fellowship with them again because their natures have not changed. I can see them and be nice, but things will never be as they once were because I know what they are capable of. Yet if you stay angry with them about whatever the situation was, you are allowing that anger to continue to keep a stronghold over you. That will keep you from growing in Christ. It can even affect your health.

I can't say that forgiving is easy. I can say it does take time. It, too, is a growth process. I am sure that many will disagree with me about the need to walk away for good from some relationships. Just make sure that you have forgiven those people in your heart. According to the Lord's Prayer, our forgiveness from God is based on our willingness to forgive. Sometimes those who have transgressed against you will keep showing up like bad pennies or a toothache. When they show up, just hold your head up and keep your distance if you have forgiven them and know that there can be no more fellowship. Don't do evil for evil. Just don't let them get to you again when you know they can't be trusted in the inner circle on "your side of the street."

Some horrible things have been done to me and said about me in the course of forty-three years of ministry. Some "church" (notice I did not say Christian) people can be mean, nasty, and downright demonic. Yet even if I don't like some of them because of their actions and ways, I have to love them just as Christ loves me. I just don't have to be in fellowship with them and open the door for them to continue ungodly actions and gossip against me. That would be like an abused person returning to the abuser and saying, "Please hurt me again." No, you forgive them, pray for them, hold your head up, and move on without wishing ill will upon them.

How to Take Care of Yourself during the Storm
You must learn to take care of yourself, especially while going through difficult times. I have noticed that when someone dies, one of the first things that happens (at least in African American communities) is that people bring food to the house of the bereaved family so that

they can focus on making arrangements and receiving visitors who come to offer condolences and so they don't forget to eat. Sorrow and grief takes your appetite away. Food doesn't taste good. However, not eating can make you weak.

A few years ago, I went through some extremely difficult experiences. Several things hit me at one time. I went about my daily routine as though I were in some kind of trance. There was a total loss of appetite. The sight of food made me sick to my stomach. All I wanted to do was to get through my tasks each day, go home, and go to bed. I lost almost one hundred pounds the wrong way. (Not that I couldn't stand to lose a few pounds.) People noticed. I had to force myself to eat something. I knew I was in a bad place in my spirit due to things that were happening on several fronts. Big storms were raging in my life. Though I will not go into detail, I had allowed people and their issues, their egos, and their quests to destroy me to become my issues.

I woke up one morning and decided that these demonic situations were not going to determine my destiny or my future. I decided to ride out the storm with dignity and to do things to take care of myself. As I mentioned earlier, when my doctor told me to find the things that make me happy and focus on them, I took his advice. I forced myself to go swimming each day, whether I felt like it or not. I joined a model railroad club (Waynesboro Model Railroad Club) almost fifty miles from my home in Greencastle, Pennsylvania, and began to construct model railroad cars and buildings and plan my layout at home. I began to take control of me.

I take my Tuesday evenings at the train club seriously. It gives me great joy, peace, and gratification to de-stress from work and church by running trains, working on the streetcar line I put in on the club layout, and creating scenery. I find that same fulfillment on Fridays, Saturdays, and Sundays after church volunteering at the Hagerstown Roundhouse Museum. I run trains, rebuild train displays and exhibits, and share my passion for trains and a little railroad history with people I meet there. I have taken several long trips to San Francisco to ride streetcars and cable cars. My passion for streetcars (trolleys, if you are from Philadelphia, Pittsburgh, and several other places) has allowed me to become a streetcar motorman at three museums. Thus, I am fulfilling my lifelong dream of being a streetcar motorman. I have now made five trips to the West Coast to ride trains, cable cars, streetcars (trolleys) LRVs (light rail vehicles, a.k.a. modern streetcars, trolley buses, and subways). Each time, God uses those trips to revive and rejuvenate my spirit. People who have no passion for a hobby would not understand the fascination connected with this hobby. Having just returned from fourteen days in California—riding San Francisco's Muni on Heritage Weekend and San Diego's MTS trolleys, and visiting the Western Railway Museum in Rio Vista and the Orange Empire Railway Museum in Perris—a peace has come over me. My blood pressure is lower, and my stress level has diminished. God enabled my friends, Dave and Wendy Housholder, to drive to San Diego and join me for a day. I even met a street evangelist in Balboa Park. I spent an hour sharing with him, and we ended up praying together.

When I started working on this book, I wrote a few pages that turned out to be part of chapter four, and then I put it aside. I did not return to it until two years ago, after my anger and resentment had subsided. I just had to focus on letting God restore my joy and my peace, which I had allowed others to steal. I took my life back from the devil. Others began to notice that I was feeling good about me again. Writing this book has been tremendously healing and therapeutic for me.

I now make no apologies for taking care of me. I just don't talk about many of my enjoyable activities anymore so that I don't open myself up to the negativity of others. It is only when you take care of yourself that you are strong enough to help others. As you take care of yourself through things that give you joy and peace, only then will you heal from your hurts. I had to make me a priority. When you become physically sick, your body focuses all of its resources on healing itself. Nothing else matters. It goes to war against infection, viruses, and whatever has made it ill. That is what you have to do for you when the storms of life hit you. Focus everything in your power on making yourself feel better physically and emotionally. Learn to laugh again. It will pay off.

Take Time for Your Family

If you are still reading this, you know from earlier chapters that my family means a great deal to me. It is a major source of encouragement and strength. If you have good relationships with family members, they are your biggest support group. Those relationships need to be nurtured and cherished. The only thing that should be a higher priority than family is your relationship with the Lord. Your family bonds will be with you during your storms, your trials, and your challenges. Family can be your sounding board for ideas, hopes, and dreams.

Do you remember that I told you that my family is my royalty? That doesn't mean that issues don't arise. It does mean that as a family, our love goes beyond our issues. When the issues arise, you should work together to resolve them as you maintain the loving relationships between family members.

Don't put your family issues out there for the world to see. Social media has hurt many families when someone uses it to air dirty family linen. Irreparable damage has been done in families and churches because some unthinking person chooses to put someone on public display. Once you say it or do it, the damage is done, and there is no way to pull it back. I have a problem with TV shows that invite people on to air their issues in front of the world.

Let's be very honest here. Every family has its issues, dirty little secrets, scars, and "blemished sheep." I have tried to be very careful not to expose any of those to the world, either in my biological family or my church family. That would not be fair to them, nor would it be good for healing, mending, or affirming relationships. God would get no glory out of it, and it would only further damage any fragile relationships. I have personally asked the permission of every person I name in this book to share statements or any part of their story that is my story.

I said earlier that I would not mention the monsters in my life by name. It would serve to validate them in my life and show that they still have control over my life. They are purposely left out. I will not discuss particular church issues or reveal where they took place because that would not be fair to those churches or families. I have to pray for them that they will also heal.

One of the greatest things you can do is to affirm members of your family. When families get together for reunions, birthdays, anniversaries, graduations, and even funerals, you have an opportunity to let each other know how important you are to each other.

I have been dubbed family historian. I made it a point as a child to listen to the family elders—even when I was not in the same room and not supposed to "be in grown folk's conversations." I listened to their wisdom and made mental notes about their handling of family issues. Sometimes when I am with younger members of my family (since I am now a senior), I share some things that happened years ago. I surprise my dad with some of the things I know and remember. My sister, nieces, daughter, and son say, "Ask my brother (or uncle or dad). He knows family stuff nobody remembers or will talk about." My sister says, "You're the keeper of the flame." I wonder sometimes who will get the "keeper of the flame" mantle when I am gone. I think my great-nephew, Darryl, is the top contender for the title. He is always asking me family questions. Usually, my niece has referred him to me. When I think about it, isn't that what was done in tribes in African and Native American cultures? Someone was responsible for the oral history.

Usually, the one asking the questions places deep value on the history and family culture. Every family has a culture, hopefully for the good.

Don't Feel Guilty about Having Some *You* Time
I make *no* apologies for the fact that, next to worship and family, I would jump over two government mules and a spotted dog for

anything to do with anything on rails. Trains have been my hobby and passion since I was three years old.

When I was three and riding in the car with my father, he pointed out a train that was passing under a bridge below us. It was the circus train arriving in the Kenilworth Avenue rail yard. I was impressed by the big steam engines pulling the train. They were belching out puffs of black smoke as the train went under us. That double-headed giant was awesome. I can remember it like it was yesterday. Now, more than six decades later, I still collect and run model trains and operate antique streetcars at several museums, living out my childhood dream. This hobby has helped me deal with the issues of life, and it gives me down time after church and work and in stressful times. I refer to my model train time as train therapy. We all need to have something that is a "de-stressor" and a buffer against the issues of life that weigh us down. God sometimes has used that time to speak to me, giving me sermons, insight on situations and how to handle them, ideas for songs, and, yes, even ideas for this book. Someone once said to me,

> Whatever your passion is beyond your walk with Christ and your family, feel free to follow it without guilt or shame. It helps to make you whole. Your *you* time can be reading a good book, cooking, entertaining, camping, swimming, cycling, or vacationing just to name a few. Whatever you enjoy that is safe and healthy helps to make you whole. Don't let the world or anything in it steal your joy from the things that give you joy. Remember that Jesus is interested in the whole person, not just the churchy part.

Writing this book has become a passion and a great part of my healing. Even though I told only a few people about it because I feared hearing negative comments, God has raised up encouraging saints along the way. Just a week ago, God raised up a new friend and prayer partner through social media in the person of Bishop Scottie Jackson (no relation other than salvation). I was about to put this project aside again, but his conversations with me and his sharing of his personal testimony and the similarity of our ministries rekindled the spark to put the finishing touches on this last chapter. Again, I could hear my grandma Graham saying, "Keep at it!"

To God Be the Glory When You Break Free and the People Feel Your Victory

It takes time to grow past obstacles and through your storms, but you will. You will survive. You will be healed. There is a song that says, "My soul looks back and wonders how I got over."

When you break free from the bondage of the things that have consumed you, you breathe a sigh of relief. You are free from the tension and stress that had its grappling hooks in your soul. Each situation that you come through gives you the strength and courage to overcome each succeeding challenge. The hymn "Yield Not to Temptation" contains the lyric, "Each victory will help you some other to win." We can only do this with God's help. When you make it through each dilemma, the trail has turned into a testimony. That testimony is a credit to the keeping power of an almighty and loving God through Christ Jesus.

I remember a situation about twenty years ago when I was going through one of the worst periods in my life. It was a very difficult time for me. I felt that there was no one I could talk to about it. Nothing could help my financial situation. I couldn't see an end to my trouble. One day, when I felt my lowest, a friend prayed with me. He thanked God for my steadfastness of faith and courage. At the end of his prayer, I told him that I didn't feel steadfast in faith, nor did I feel courageous.

His response was, "You don't see what we (your friends) see. You have no idea how many people are watching you weather this storm. You have encouraged so many by the way you are going through your trial."

When the situation eventually got better, people told me that I showed great courage and strength. They told me of others who had gained strength to deal with their situations because of me. It was a humbling experience, and I will never forget it. I learned from it that others are watching your walk even when you don't know it. Your walk is your testimony.

Just a few years ago, a series of storms came upon me. I could only think of Job's situation. Each storm could have caused me to give up. However, God showered me with His comfort and peace. It was He, the Lord, Who brought me through each situation that has been resolved. Some are still working themselves out with God's help and grace.

These were "*keep at it*" moments. I would get up each day and force myself to go about my daily tasks as though nothing was wrong. I would go home not wanting to eat because even looking at food made me sick. I just wanted to curl up in a ball in bed. The only thing I could say to God in prayer was, "Oh, Jesus, I hurt! Oh, God, what did I do that caused these monsters to work against me?"

I was in a state of spiritual warfare with monsters in my life that just wouldn't let up. If I thought about or looked at the demonic forces working against me, I just wanted to vomit. But God showed me that He would be with me. I just had to hold on to Him in the midst of the adversity. I had to keep at it—keep my faith and trust in Him. What a relief it was for Him to bring me through it. What a humbling experience it was for me to see others stand with me in prayer. The Lord is a deliverer and a healer. I had to hold on to Christ's keeping power with every part of my being as I held my head up high each day. I just had to *keep at it.*

When other bad situations come upon me, I think of how God brought me through that tough time, and I know that whatever I am facing at that moment, He will get me through it. He has done it many times before. I start to rejoice while I am going through those storms because I know by faith that He will bring me out of them. He is that kind of God, and Christ is just that kind of savior. I don't know what I will go through in the future. I may experience more sorrow at some point, but the Lord will see me through. I may experience difficult challenges, but I won't give up on myself or on the things God wants me to accomplish. In the words of my grandmother, I will just *keep at it*!

As I said, my mother used to say, "A job worth doing is worth doing well." My sister and I had that drilled into us. Homework was never turned in sloppy. You had to redo it. The dishes had to be done correctly, along with the vacuuming, the dusting, and the setting of the dinner table when company was coming. With my dad, the grass had to be cut a certain way. What that taught my sister and me was that we are to take pride in our work and have a good work ethic.

Don't give up on your hopes, dreams, and ideas. No matter who or what the obstacles are, just keep at it.